David Mortimer

CLASSIC RUGBY CLANGERS

Fluffs, fails and foul-ups from the world's rugby pitches

PORTICO

First published in the United Kingdom in 2015 by
Portico
1 Gower Street
London
WC1E 6HD

An imprint of Pavilion Books Company Ltd

ISBN 978-1-91023-207-1

A CIP catalogue record for this book is available from the British Library.

10 9 8 7 6 5 4 3 2 1

Reproduction by Mission Productions Ltd, Hong Kong
Printed and bound by CPI Group (UK) Ltd, Croydon, CR0 4YY

This book can be ordered direct from the publisher at www.pavilionbooks.com

Contents

This book is dedicated to all those husbands, wives, partners, sons, daughters or parents who have ever patrolled a muddy touchline in sleet or rain wondering which of the thirty meandering mudstacks on the pitch is theirs.

The author would like to pay tribute to Donald McRae's excellent book Winter Colours, *which inspired a couple of pieces in this book. Any rugby fan who hasn't already had the good fortune to read it is guaranteed a lot of future pleasure.*

Foreword

Mike Gibson, the great Irish and Lions fly-half and centre of the 1960s and 1970s, once singled out self-confidence as the quality most needed by rugby players. The only thing worse than a lack of self-confidence, he said, was a misplaced self-confidence. In effect, he was describing the potential choker and the potential joker. On the one hand there is the player who, however great his skills, experiences a moment of crisis in which self-doubt leads to erroneous decision-making or a tension-induced tightening of the nerves that can be sufficient to fluff the kick or the pass. On the other hand is the player who, in a moment of hubris, lets his concentration and application slip and commits what seems an almost casual blunder. Either way, the mistake may pass unnoticed or, if the victim is unlucky, it will be the very public error which appears to give the game away. As spectators, we are rarely neutral. We take sides, and our adrenalin flows with the tide of the contest. When our team wins we celebrate the obvious and visible heroes, whether George North for a blistering try or Jonny Wilkinson for a nerveless kick, and chronicle them accordingly. When we lose, we groan over the poor performances of X, Y or Z but, maybe through sympathy for the underdog, we only occasionally heap opprobrium on one unfortunate player.

One of the great attractions of sport is the interplay of human skills and emotions that it displays, and the way the participants rise or, sometimes, fall to the occasion; and the greater that occasion, the greater the pressure exerted on the players. Since rugby is a game concentrated into just eighty minutes, with laws in a state of seemingly constant revision in order to speed things up, rapidity of thought and action is essential, and the margins of error grow ever finer. Yet as the media searchlight, television in particular, probes the game – even the depths of that old mystery, the scrum – ever more insistently, the more a single failure of nerve, judgement, temperament or skill is exposed.

This little book celebrates some of rugby's red-faced moments drawn from 140 years or more of its history, and while it certainly puts names to the blushing faces, be they of individuals, teams or officials, it has absolutely no desire to shame them. Not only have most of them suffered enough already, but they were generally giving their all when the clanger was dropped, and in most cases those very same individuals or teams provided us with many more hours of pleasure than of cursing. Affection with, maybe, some occasional gentle humour is the order of the day!

Before the Old Farts Sounded Off

How rugby and its scoring system developed, 1871 onwards

'The past,' said L P Hartley, 'is a foreign country. They do things differently there.' Of all the games that emerged from chaos into regulation during the long Victorian era, it could be argued that rugby has sustained more subsequent change and alteration than any other. If we could travel back and stand on a rugby touchline over 130 years ago, we would struggle to recognise the game being played, and would need a wet towel round the head to unravel its scoring system.

The great public schools of the early nineteenth century all encouraged games loosely based on the football that had been played in towns and villages for many generations. Back in 1581, the headmaster of St Paul's School in London saw positive educational values in football, while also recognising the 'abuse and violence' associated with the game. And what he meant by football was closer to rugby than to soccer for, as subsequent accounts describe, catching and running with the ball was a key part of the sport. So when William Webb Ellis allegedly picked up the ball and ran with it he was probably not acting outside the rules, such as they were, of a game called football, but at worst infringing the rules peculiar to his own school's version of the game. As he died a minister of the church, he had clearly repented of whatever it was he did.

Indeed, it was soccer, not rugby, that broke from the traditions of the ancient game called football when, in 1863, the recently formed Football Association sought to outlaw running, handling and mauling (the laws codified by Rugby School) in favour of dribbling with the feet (as codified by Eton School – which prompts the thought that soccer might have come to be called eton!). The Blackheath club was so upset by this proposition, and by its accompanying suggestion that you should be allowed to hack the shins only of the player with the ball, that it walked out, and by 1871 the Rugby Football Union had come into being. Thereafter, yard by painful yard, rugby shoved its way towards the game we know and love today, although for some time yet the number of players in a side was twenty, thirteen of whom were in the scrummage, and in this all-embracing scrum the ball could remain a thing of rarely sighted mystery to long-suffering spectators (although followers of England in the mid-1990s could be forgiven for thinking how little had changed in a century).

Kicking skills remained highly prized, and the scoring system reflected this. Initially, a touchdown gave the side that had achieved it the right to 'try' (hence the name) to kick a goal (the modern conversion). The touchdown itself counted for nothing and earned no numerical recognition. It was the dropped goal that carried the greatest kudos. When, in the 1880s, Yorkshire outplayed Middlesex, creating four tries (but failing to convert any of them to goals) and were then beaten by a dropped goal from Andrew Stoddart, the England cricket and rugby captain, the outcry was so great that the rules were subsequently changed. Even so, the dropped goal retained its supremacy as the most valuable single scoring opportunity, carrying four points, right up until its devaluation to the modern three points in 1948.

In 1886 the RFU finally adopted a points system (which at first the other home countries refused to accept): a try was allotted one point, and a successful goal – i.e. conversion – a further two points. Having stepped onto this dangerous bandwagon of allowing points for mere handling skills, the RFU was unable to alight. As soon as 1892 it found itself upping the value of the try to two points (and to three for a conversion) and then to three in 1894 (the conversion deflating again to two). This gave the running game its final licence, and while foot rushes by packs of forwards continued to evoke admiration and excitement, by the time World War I enforced a hiatus in sporting affairs, the 'twinkling runs' of three-quarters like Ronnie Poulton and Cyril Lowe were what the crowds longed to see. Thereafter, the balance between foot and hand reflected in the scoring system stayed unchanged, excepting only the 1948 dropped-goal amendment, until 1971, when a try became four points, before being extended again in 1992 to its current five. In general, though, the frequency with which the laws are amended and tidied up is a useful reminder that the game of rugby is ever-changing and, whatever our 21st-century views, when we revisit the past we have to remind ourselves how differently they did things then.

A Triumph For Advocates of Noise Abatement

Scotland v England, Edinburgh, March 1871

Banish any idea that rugby's first international was a spiffing wheeze to have a weekend jolly in Edinburgh. The Scots had issued the invitation with one idea, and one only, in mind – victory, and proof that England's 1–0 victory in a soccer match between the two countries a year before was an irrelevance. The game was to be twenty a side, fifty minutes each way and, since different sets of laws existed either side of the Tweed, it would be played under Scottish rules. No settled scoring system yet existed. A try counted for nothing other than qualifying the side that made it to 'try' a kick at goal.

Before battle commenced, it was agreed that 'no hacking-over or tripping-up should be allowed, and that the ball should not be taken up for a run unless absolutely bounding, as opposed to rolling.' If that seemed to emasculate the contest a trifle, at least everyone knew where they stood or, as events were to prove, thought they did. The first half was even and scoreless, but soon after the restart the Englishmen made their fatal blunder and forgot whose laws they were playing under.

After a maul on the English goal line, the two umpires who patrolled the touchlines (a single referee came later) decreed a five-yard scrum. 'Instead of putting it down,' a later account said, 'the Scottish forwards drove the entire scrummage into goal and grounded the ball.' According to English laws, this was illegal but, starting their international history as they meant to go on, the English had been caught napping by the wily old Scots.

English protests were long and loud, and the two umpires met in solemn conclave to consider them but, as one of them wrote much later, 'I do not know whether the decision was correct. When an umpire is in doubt, he is justified in deciding against the side which makes most noise. They are probably in the wrong.' Overlooking the point that Scotland, as the beneficiaries, were unlikely to make much noise on that occasion, one can only feel relieved for the umpires' sake that Neil Back's great-grandfather was not playing that day (see page 132).

If It's No Trouble, Could You Turn Out For England Today?
Ireland v England, Dublin, 1880

It took Ireland a while to settle into rugby at international level, even though they had formed the IFU in 1874. Thanks to internal squabbling between Dublin and Belfast, a novel solution had to be reached to produce a team of twenty to play England in London in February 1875. Dublin would select half the side and Belfast the rest. Since 15-a-side rugby was the norm in Ireland, whereas twenty remained *de rigueur* in England, it was hardly surprising that those of the Irish team who actually turned up for the game had little idea in what position they were supposed to be playing. Moreover, in the immortal words of Jacques McCarthay, they 'were immaculately innocent of training', while two of the team had other plans than rugby in mind. H B Robinson used the match as a pretext to visit his relatives, and W B Smyth thought a spot of sightseeing a preferable activity. Ireland lost heavily, of course.

This endearing trait of turning out for the old country if you had nothing better to do recurred in 1880 when England crossed the Irish Sea for the fixture at Lansdowne Road, though this time the boot was on the other foot. In those days, the players paid their own way, and generally travelled at the last moment by the cheapest means. The crossing was rough and a number of the English players were seasick, so England made enquiries at Trinity College and unearthed Ernie Woodward, an English student who, fortunately, reckoned he could spare a couple of hours. It was perhaps a pity that he was unable to make Trinity's second XV, but as Ireland had yet to score a single point against England in five attempts, it probably wouldn't matter.

As indeed it didn't. On this occasion, Ireland did at least succeed in touching down under the posts, and fullback Dolway Walkington stepped up for the conversion. The eccentric Walkington sported a monocle when playing rugby, which he would remove before attempting a tackle. Presumably he also removed it for this historic kick, and was unable to see the posts, since he missed. It would be seven more years before Ireland at last beat England.

Wind Gathers in the Nether Regions

English and Scottish officialdom get a teeny bit pompous, 1889–1936

'Man, proud man, dressed in a little brief authority.' How could Shakespeare have foreseen with such insight how a rugby official would behave three centuries later; and how could rugby, of all sports, surround itself with governing bodies of such narrow-minded pomposity almost from its earliest days? The (English) Rugby Football Union was founded in 1871 and thereafter, despite Irish claims to the contrary, insisted that it had invented rugby (hence the need – once the gentleman in question was safely deceased – to create the Webb Ellis myth). It was a short step, quickly taken by the RFU, from claiming invention of the game to ownership of it, and from ownership to insisting that nobody else's opinion counted, irrespective of playing merit. Thus, for example, South Africans, New Zealanders and Australians were colonials who were jolly lucky to be allowed to play against English sides – notwithstanding that, in no time, they were inflicting regular drubbings on them and, indeed, every other northern hemisphere team.

Typical of this attitude was the behaviour of Rowland Hill in and after the match between the New Zealand Natives and England at Blackheath in February 1889. Hill was not the chap who invented postage stamps, but he was the secretary of the RFU and therefore, in his own eyes, at least as important. It was therefore extraordinarily gracious of him to agree to take the whistle for this international match. Towards the end of the first half, the ball twice went loose behind New Zealand's posts. On each occasion, New Zealand touched it down for a five-yard scrum, only for England's Harry Bedford to fall on it. On each occasion, Hill awarded a try. In the second half, Andrew Stoddart's shorts were ripped in the tackle by New Zealand's Tom Ellison and, while attention was diverted by the enthralling spectacle of order and decency being restored to Stoddart's nether regions, England's Frank Evershed picked up the ball and stole over to claim a try, which Mr Hill unhesitatingly awarded. Three of the visitors walked off in protest, and all diplomatic hell broke loose. The RFU (i.e. Mr Hill) had been insulted. An apology must be given, in writing and in a form acceptable to the RFU (i.e. Mr Hill). The first attempt was unacceptable to the RFU (i.e. Mr Hill) and the matter was resolved only when he, Mr Hill, had dictated the apology that Mr Hill condescended to accept.

The penalty for daring to question the almighty RFU was more than a mere apology could satisfy. The New Zealanders were socially ostracised for the rest of the tour and, when it was time for the voyage home, there was no official party to say farewell. The RFU doubtless wished to echo Jane Austen's Lady Catherine de Bourgh, and say: 'I take no leave of you. You deserve no such attention. I am most seriously displeased.' Had the New Zealander's ship been under sail, the RFU's collective breaking of wind would probably have got it most of the way home.

But if English officialdom was rigid, it necessarily followed that the Scottish RU must outdo them, and the 'frosty-faced conservatism' of their secretary J Aikman Smith after World War I would be hilarious in other circumstances. It was Smith who, famously, brought only fourteen shirts to Scotland's first international after the war on the grounds that Jock Wemyss, who had lost an eye in action, had played before 1914, and therefore already had one. Dammit, man, keeping your shirt washed and pressed is more important than beating the Germans! Not until 1936, many years after all other teams, did Smith allow numbers rather than letters on the players' backs ('a rugby match, not a cattle sale').

The SRU's ability to keep a grudge warm was especially spectacular. The 1905 All Blacks had toured Britain on condition they were paid their daily expenses, and although Scotland had reluctantly overlooked 'shamateurism' on that occasion (they lost 12–7), not even the intervention of the Great War – in which Scotland lost many of its capped players – was allowed to put this iniquity to rest. When the All Blacks visited Britain again, two decades later, Mr Smith and his colleagues were still chuntering self-righteously, and

Scotland refused to play them. To this day, the Scots are paying the penalty for this boneheadedness. If there was ever a year in which they might have beaten the Blacks it was 1925, the year in which Scotland produced what many still think was its finest team, and one that achieved the Grand Slam (see page 46). As it is, they have never beaten New Zealand.

Hasie Versfeld Makes His Point

British Isles v Cape Town Clubs, Cape Town, July 1891

The first rugby clubs began to appear in South Africa in 1875, and by 1889 they were ready to form the South African Rugby Football Board and press for a visit from the old country. That same year a group of English cricketers had been invited to the Cape to teach the locals a few tricks of the trade, and had won every single game of a lengthy itinerary with disarming ease. Clearly the colonials had a suitably humble attitude towards improving their game, and that being so the English RFU felt moved to comply.

The party that went to South Africa was made up of Englishmen and Scots captained by Bill Maclagan, of whom the *Cape Times* wrote: 'He has acquired the acme of perfection as a tackler, and can cover the ground at a splendid pace.' The Cambridge centre R L Aston, 'the best passing man in England', also made a deep impression. Maclagan's team embarked on a programme of nineteen games, of which three were classified as internationals.

Like the cricketers, the rugby players swept all before them on a tour described by one of the group, Paul Clauss, as 'all champagne and travel' but – and this is when they dropped an unpardonable clanger – they conceded a point. It's true they amassed 224 themselves but, in their very first game against Cape Town Clubs, they allowed Charles 'Hasie' Versfeld to score a try. 'Versfeld found an opening, put in a grand sprint and scored a try amidst tremendous cheering. Duff took the kick, but failed to announce the major points.' Hasie became a national hero overnight and set the Springboks on the road to establishing rugby as a religion. To be sure, Maclagan didn't let it happen again. When, in a game against Transvaal, someone sneaked over the line, he picked him up bodily and dumped him out of play before he could touch down. But the South Africans were quick learners. It took only twelve years for them to beat the British Isles when, after two drawn Tests in 1903, they won the decider at Newlands 8–0. Today, South Africa's rugby HQ in Pretoria is named after Hasie's brother, Loftus Versfeld.

Louis Magee's Match

Wales v Ireland, Cardiff, 1899

The Triple Crown was recognised for the first time in 1899 as the term for a clean sweep of all the home unions, and Ireland were the first to wear it. Just as Jackie Kyle was to be the Irish hero when they did the Grand Slam in 1948, so their brilliant fly-half Louis Magee lifted the crown for them almost half a century earlier. Resourceful, daring, quick and determined in attack, he played 27 times for them between 1895 and 1904, but his greatest moment was a defensive one, at Cardiff in 1899.

Ireland led, and eventually won, by a single score – a try from their wing G P Doran just before half-time. This was the day that play was suspended because of a pitch invasion. The crowd was so great, and so excited, that the railings gave way and it spilled on to the pitch 'like water from a broken dam'. Billy Bancroft of Wales was so badly hurt in the human flood that 'the subsequent proceedings interested him no more', and he retired from the game.

Order was eventually restored and, with minutes remaining, a sweeping Welsh passing movement between Selwyn Biggs, Llewellyn Lloyd and Gwyn Nicholls opened up the Irish defence and put centre R T Skrimshire away. Skrimshire had many virtues but one big defect. 'Chivalrous unselfishness was far from him. He starved his wings, he wanted to do it all.' Skrimshire had the line at his mercy and Willie Llewellyn unmarked outside him when Magee, 'coming up like a whirlwind', hauled him down from behind a few feet short of the line. Magee had saved his country and ensured them the brand new Triple Crown. To be fair to Skrimshire, as few of his countrymen felt disposed to be at the time, he could not have seen Magee closing from behind, but his reputation as a selfish player worked against him, and the three caps he won in 1899 were destined to be his only ones.

It's All Rather Confusing, Really

Wales v New Zealand, Cardiff, December 1905

Half a century after the famous 1905 All Blacks suffered their first international reverse, 3–0 at the hands of Wales, Neddy Seagoon, the antihero of radio's famous *Goon Show*, coined the catch-phrase 'It's all rather confusing, really.' As a Welshman, Seagoon's alter ego, Harry Secombe, might well have been drawing on the folk memory of John Dewar Dallas, the referee for this memorable match. Dallas was a stripling of 27, younger than some of the players in the game, who had played for Scotland against England at Twickenham only two years earlier and scored a try. This makes it all the more puzzling that he turned out to referee the All Black match in street clothes and boots without bars or studs, with the predictable result that he was often to be found a long way behind the play. This was to give rise to one of the most hotly debated phantom tries in the game's history, and leave Dallas scarlet with embarrassment or (in New Zealand eyes) guilt.

The All Blacks began their inexorable quest for international rugby supremacy in 1903. The following year they beat a British Isles team 9–3 in Wellington and when, in September 1905, after their first team had already left for the tour of Britain, their second XV beat Australia, local cartoonists were already depicting New Zealand as World Champions. Their progress through Britain seemed to confirm this view as they won all but one of their 32 tour games, scoring 830 points against a mere 39 in reply. The one they didn't win, and it remains a sore point to this day, was against Wales.

The whole thing began with something of an unresolved mystery. Missing from the All Black side that day was one of their key players, Billy Stead, master tactician and stand-off half, who had been pivotal in the defeats of Scotland, Ireland and England. In one account he was the victim of dysentery, in another of a heavy cold; then again, it might have been boils or, as one version insisted, H J Mynott wanted a game, so Stead stood down to let him have it. If so, it was a bad decision. Mynott had a shocker.

According to British accounts, the Welsh won because their forwards 'proved themselves the equals of the New Zealanders in obtaining possession of the ball in the scrummage'. The view from down under was that the referee penalised Dave Gallaher every time he put the ball into the scrum so that he ordered his hooker not to strike but to let Wales have possession. Take your pick. Either way, the Welsh had such regular ball that they were almost constantly attacking, and eventually came away with a first-half try from Teddy Morgan on the left wing.

At the heart of the disputed second-half 'try that wasn't' was 21-year-old Bob Deans. Deans was wealthy, deeply religious and teetotal, as well as immensely generous and fun-loving but, only three years later, he would be dead. Wales had won a lineout and kicked ahead to Billy Wallace on the All Blacks' left wing. Wallace ran diagonally into the Welsh half, side-stepped one player, cut between two more and raced up to the 25 where fullback Winfield was waiting for him. According to his own account, he was debating the respective merits of a chip ahead or a dummy when he heard Deans outside him yelling, 'I'm with you!' Wallace threw a long pass, Deans gathered cleanly, veered in towards the posts, then out again as he saw Morgan racing across from the left wing. Had he not swung inwards, he would have had ample time to score. As it was, Wallace maintained that 'he grounded the ball six inches over the line' as Rhys Gabe tackled him.

The referee was a long way away and, well before he arrived on the scene, Deans got up. Had he remained lying on the ball, legend would have been robbed of one of its enduring controversies but, by the time Mr Dallas came panting up, he was already being offered Welsh and Kiwi versions of where the ball had been grounded. Morgan later said Deans had scored, whereas Gabe said he had not. When he had got his breath back the referee announced Deans had been held up and awarded a five-yard scrum. Despite the protagonists being long dead, the controversy rumbled on for most of the twentieth century but, as Chester and McMillan said in their book *Men in Black*: 'The whole incident is rather confusing.'

That's My Boy!

Ireland v South Africa, Belfast, November 1906

No sooner had the 1905 All Blacks departed than the home unions, clearly enjoying the masochistic frisson of defeat at colonial hands, prepared to greet the first Springboks. Scotland welcomed their light forwards and handling backs to Hampden Park with a waterlogged pitch ('Grand weather for drooning the Boks') and won 6–0. It was the last international the South Africans would lose in Britain until 1965!

Their next Test, against Ireland, was played in much better conditions and produced a thrilling game which, at that early point in the international catalogue, was reckoned to be one of the most exciting in history. At half-time, the Springboks led 12–3, having scored three tries and a penalty, and appeared to have the game under complete control. In those days half-time meant no more than a five-minute break on the pitch, and the Irish must have been treated to some fiery Celtic exhortations because, in the second half, it was all Ireland. First, a penalty pulled the score back to 12–6. Then came Basil Maclear's try, 'which would in itself have sufficed to make the match memorable in the annals of great games'. Scooping the ball up, he nearly fell over himself but, despite floundering as he tried to hit his stride, managed to beat several Springboks. Fullback Stevie Joubert should have had his man but, with a vigorous hand-off, Maclear sent him sprawling and the score was 12–9. Within minutes it was level, as Ireland wheeled a scrum and took the ball over the line in a foot-rush.

Only in recent times have neutral touch judges been selected. Back in those sporting days, 'when even spectators knew how to accept defeat with generosity', each side would provide one judge, and running the line for the Springboks that day was 'Klondike' Raaff, one of their own playing party. With only minutes left, Anton Stegmann broke down the touchline for a long run in to score the decisive try. Running alongside him, Raaff hurled his flag in the air with a whoop of delight, and Ireland came to a halt assuming a foot in touch. No such luck! The try stood, and the Springboks had sealed the match 15–12.

If the Cap Fits

Just a few of the men who weren't invited back, 1906, 1970, 1993, 1994 & 1892

Dr Arnold Alcock, of Guy's Hospital and Blackheath, was enjoying his buttered toast for breakfast as he opened a letter from the secretary of the RFU inviting him, if he had no other plans, to turn out for England against South Africa on Saturday. The good doctor was surprised and flattered, and turned out to such effect that England drew 3–3 their first home encounter with the colonials in 1906. Before doing so he had, however, caused the worthy secretary's heart to miss a few beats since he had really meant to send the invitation to Andrew Slocock. Modern revisionists suspect Alcock was the intended victim all along but, whether or not the doctor appeared under false pretences, he wasn't asked back, and thus became an early addition to the long list of those whose appearances for their country have become stuck at the number one.

Just about the unluckiest player ever to win a single cap was Maestag's Chico Hopkins, and even that was for a mere fifteen minutes' work as he came on against England at Twickenham in 1970. Hopkins had the singular misfortune to be contemporary with the great Gareth Edwards, and spent most of his career sitting on the subs bench waiting for Gareth to pull something painful. Alas for Hopkins, that England game was the only occasion on which he was obliging enough to do so. Wales were trailing 6–13, and 'their play was shot with desperation', when Chico arrived to sort things out. His 'immaculate rolling kicks' quickly led to a try to give Wales hope and, in the dying seconds, he scored himself to give Wales a breathless win by 17–13. Fifteen minutes of immaculate conception, and he was popped back into the womb of the subs bench for ever.

At least Colin Wilkinson managed the full eighty minutes for Ireland against Scotland in 1993 and, as he was already looking out his zimmer frame at the advanced age of 31, he might have been grateful for even the one cap at fullback. Former Ulster coach Ken Reid reckoned that Wilkinson 'liked his beer, and he liked to enjoy himself. He was really a sportsman from another age, before it all got serious.' On the day, the weather was appalling, and the game became one of those dour, wet-weather struggles between the packs which Scotland won 15–3. The selectors forgot to send him his cap, which seemed a trifle mean as they clearly weren't intent on giving him a chance to start a collection but, once the press got hold of the story, the cap turned up in Wilkinson's post in double-quick time.

The Springboks brought in Orange Free State prop Andre-Henry Le Roux for his first cap against England in 1994, but he lasted only one game. It's asking a lot of the Broederbond to take to a player with a name like Andre-Henry; or perhaps he couldn't stomach the flavour of ear (see page 120), but next time out his namesake Johan was preferred. It hadn't helped, of course, that England won 32–15.

To find a truly spectacular one-cap wonder we must go back to Victorian times, and a game between Wales and England that would have been a 14-all draw, but for the sniffy attitude of the other home unions faced with Wales's sensible suggestion that the new scoring system of 1892 (two points for a try, three for a conversion) should be altered to three for a try and two for the kick – as it was a year later. Had England agreed, they would have had a draw, but their refusal cost them the match 12–11. Halfback Howard Marshall was making his debut for England, and he could scarcely have invented a more heroic start to his international career. With England 2–0 ahead, he scooped the ball from his forwards' heels and darted over for a converted try to put England 7–0 ahead at half-time. Shortly after the restart, he made a swerving, solo run to stretch the lead to 9–0, before a Welsh fightback made it 9–7. From an English heel in the Welsh 25, Marshall stretched the lead with his third try, only for Arthur Gould to keep Wales in touch at 11–9 with a successful effort of his own. Then, in the very last minute, Wales won a penalty out on the far left-hand touchline. Ignoring his captain's plea to take a proper and respectful place kick, Billy Bancroft calmly drop-kicked it safely between the posts to see Wales home, 12–11. Marshall, who had all but given England victory, was rewarded for his heroics with the information that henceforth he need expect no future letters of invitation from the secretary of the RFU.

A Promising Career Cut Short by a Sandwich

Sad stories of missed international honours, 1911–69

Rugby history is rich in jokers who contrived to pass up the international caps they might have won but for circumstances that, with a little more care, they could have avoided. In 1911, Gaston Vareilles was on his way to Paris to play for France in their first-ever home international against Scotland, of which Reuters was to report that 'no finer match has ever been seen in France'. Promptly at 2.30, the Scots made a great impression by sending a kilted piper ahead to play them onto the pitch 'amid great cheering'. There followed some delay before the French straggled out and, when they did, it was quickly apparent that they had less than an ample sufficiency for the purposes of playing rugby. Vareilles had disappeared, and they had only fourteen men. Up in the stands, meanwhile, Andre Franquenelle, the French sprinter, was impatiently awaiting kickoff when it was announced that, most regrettably, France were a man short. Without waiting to ask for his entrance money back, Franquenelle volunteered and had rather a good game as France achieved the first international victory in their history by 16–15. What had happened to Gaston Vareilles? Feeling a trifle peckish, he had jumped off his train to buy a sandwich at a country station. We all know what the service can be like in a station buffet, and it's unlikely things were that much better back in 1911. By the time he turned round with the sandwich in his hand, the train was a mile or two down the line, and not even a man selected to play on the wing could expect to overhaul it. He did eventually make it to the dressing-room door and was told, with the stunning brevity of which the French language is capable, where to go. He never played for France again, while Franquenelle won another two caps!

Three years later, Dickie Lloyd was selected to play for Ireland against Wales in Belfast. He came out onto the pitch beforehand with the rest of the team for a pre-match photograph, and thought it might be a good idea to get into match fitness by jogging round the field before kickoff. Such strenuous activity was his undoing. He pulled a muscle and had to be replaced, although he did eventually win nineteen caps and was a respected opponent.

Jean-Pierre Salut's heart undoubtedly beat with patriotic fervour when he was told of his selection for France against Scotland at the Stade de Colombes in 1969. Little did he know that, however unwittingly, he was about to enter the record books. Come the great day, he prepared to run out from the changing rooms underneath the stand following his fourteen colleagues. Along the corridor they ran, and up a flight of steps to the pitch. As he reached the top step he tripped and broke his ankle, becoming the only player in the history of international rugby to be carried off the pitch before actually stepping onto it. Happily, further opportunities came his way.

Which is more than can be said for Tommy England, who was selected for Wales in 1890 but was injured before the big day. He was replaced by Billy Bancroft, who went on to become one of the earliest Welsh legends, wining 33 consecutive caps. In despair, England retired, uncapped. Nearly half a century later, Charles Anderson, Harry Edwards and Tom Stone were all picked by Wales to play against Ireland at Lansdowne Road in 1937, but the game was postponed because of heavy fog, all three were dropped and never selected again. Another half-century later saw Graham Dawe win his third cap for England against Wales (1987). In his three games he had, in John Reason's words, 'done some things that have been quite daft, and has been more than lucky not to have been sent off.' This game produced one of the most notorious punch-ups in which English and Welsh forwards indulged around this time, and while Dawe was not dismissed he was later suspended. Brian Moore came in as his replacement, and Dawe spent almost the rest of his career on the substitutes' bench.

The accolade for sheer panache in becoming an early one-cap wonder unquestionably goes to Bert Solomon. Picked for England in the first international ever to be played at Twickenham, in January

1910, Solomon made an impressive debut against Wales, whom England had not beaten since 1898. Major Philip Trevor, doyen of the day's rugby correspondents, described how, with the game delicately balanced, 'Solomon made a capital run'. He dummied a pass to the right, feinted left, swerved inwards and scored. England won 11–6, whereupon Solomon, pre-empting any risk of selectorial eccentricity, declared himself well satisfied with his international career. Henceforth, he let it be known, he would be content to be left in peace down in Redruth.

Watts Up Now?

England v Wales, Twickenham, January 1914

'Lucky' Twickenham, they called it. After its international inauguration in 1910, England had yet to be beaten there, thanks in part to several instances of good fortune. England had beaten Wales for the Grand Slam in 1913, and it was correctly forecast that the 1914 campaign might well be decided by the contest between the Welsh forwards and the English backs in the opening international of the season. England won 10–9 and did indeed go on to their second consecutive Grand Slam.

The *Illustrated Sporting News* could hardly contain its indignation. England 'had all the worst of the play, and for quite two-thirds of the game had been on the defensive. Their undoubtedly brilliant three-quarters had been quite unable to get going, for the simple reason that five times out of six their forwards were beaten for a possession and their system of attack had been reduced to impotence.' Not that the *News* was partial in its scorn. 'Wales has turned out some bad three-quarter lines of late years, but this was easily the worst of the lot,' it fumed, before returning to lambast 'the English hooker, whoever he may have been, who seemed to be stricken with the palsy'.

What went wrong for Wales? Willie Watts. He was winning his first and, as it transpired, his last cap for Wales, and in the second half he experienced a lifetime's-worth of mixed emotions. England led 5–4 at the interval, but soon after the restart Ronnie Poulton's clearance kick was charged down, Watts scooped up the loose ball and ran in unopposed for a try, converted by Billie Bancroft to give Wales a 9–5 lead.

As Welsh forward domination continued, England's cause seemed doomed until 'all the good fortune they have enjoyed at Twickenham paled into insignificance beside the gift vouchsafed to them in the closing stages.' With Wales defending in their own 25, Watts took his eye off the ball and let it bounce right into the path of England's redoubtable No 8, 'Cherry' Pillman, who hoofed it over the line and won the desperate race to touch down. Poor Willie Watts had, effectively, scored at both ends.

The Irish Cordially Invite Their Welsh Friends to a Fight

Ireland v Wales, Belfast, February 1914

Let's get the score out of the way before we start. While the forwards were otherwise preoccupied, the Welsh backs beat the Irish backs in the rugby-playing part of the entertainment by 11–3.

Newport's Percy Jones was a member of the Welsh pack, the 'Terrible Eight' as they were afterwards christened, who travelled to Belfast for the 1914 game with Ireland. On the Friday night, he went to the theatre with his Newport teammate Harry Uzzell, and a couple of the Irish team. Over came Dr (later to become Sir Walter) Tyrrell, the leader of the Irish pack. 'Here, Uzzell,' he said to Harry, 'where's this Percy Jones you've got about with you? I'll have a go at him tomorrow.' 'All right,' replied Percy, 'I'm a Welshman, and I'll be with you.' It was all quite pally, but that was how it started, Jones recalled in later years.

Let Percy carry on the story: 'We didn't have to wait long before the fireworks started. In the first few minutes Tyrrell got me, and everything inside my head rattled. Then Abraham, the Irish centre, kept having a go at me as well; and so I called Uzzell: "You'd better come with me; there's another bloke at it now."' At half-time, Tyrrell came across and informed Jones that he reckoned he was two up, which Jones agreed. Leading the Welsh pack, Uzzell decided to play the Irish at their own game, and his forwards eagerly agreed. 'The play that followed,' said Percy, 'was easily the fiercest I ever saw or took part in. There was no squealing, by us or them, and after the game, too, we were the best of pals. Even Tyrrell gave in at last. "You're the best Welshman I've ever run across," he said to me. "You are the only man who ever beat me."' The match was followed by 'the friendliest of dinners'. Jones and Tyrrell sat together and signed each other's menus as a memento of what was quickly dubbed 'The

Roughest Match' of all time! In the centre of a subsequent photo of the Terrible Eight sits the most pugnacious-looking of the lot – the Reverend J Alban Davies. Muscular Christianity personified.

Come On In,
the Water's Lovely

New Zealand v South Africa, Wellington, September 1921

The Springboks' first visit to New Zealand in 1921 generated enormous excitement. Each side regarded itself – with justification – as the best in the business and this series, intended to decide who was top gun, was played with 'the raw intensity and fierce physical commitment that were to mark all subsequent contests'. The All Blacks won the first encounter 13–5, while the Springboks ground their way to a remorseless 9–5 victory in the second.

For several weeks before the all-important third Test, the ground was hard and the weather more like summer than winter, but the evening before the match, the rain fell and fell, and went on falling. Surviving photographs show bow waves of water spraying knee-high, so it was hardly surprising that the game was confined mainly to the forwards and that opportunities for the lively backs on both sides were few and far between. Nevertheless, Jack Steel, on New Zealand's right wing, 'made some grand runs', and towards the end of the first half, left wing Keith Siddells 'broke away with the ball at his feet, but lost control when he struck a pool of water'. Better – or worse – was to come.

The All Blacks began to pin the Springboks into their own half, and only their great fullback, Gerhard Morkel, looked capable of delaying the inevitable score. Midway through the second half, the Blacks finally opened the door. The ball was whipped back to fly-half Billy Fea. He dropped it, but Steel gathered it in and raced up the touchline. Beating two tackles, he seemed to have the line at his mercy when a small lake loomed in his path. Steel went in and left it at speed, but whereas he entered in an orthodox position, he emerged flat on his back, the ball squirting out of his hands as he did so. There was one last chance. Centre Mark Nicholls found

Steel unmarked outside him but, presumably unwilling to chance another exhibition of aquaplaning, he cut in and was buried by the Springbok forwards. The final score of 0–0 meant the two teams would wait another sixteen years (see page 54) to decide which of them was the greatest.

Wakefield Has a Distressing Season

1921–2 was not a season to remember

The great Wavell Wakefield was not accustomed to things going wrong in a distinguished career, which included three Grand Slams between 1921 and 1924, but, as if to prove the impartiality of fate, he was taught more than one painful lesson in the space of a few months in the winter of 1921–2. Going up to Cambridge in the autumn of 1921, he won his blue that December in a powerful pack, including internationals Geoff Conway and Ronnie Cove-Smith, which was expected to overwhelm Oxford. Before the match, both teams were staying in Eastbourne: Cambridge at the Cavendish Hotel, and Oxford at the Grand. Dreaming up a jolly jape, Wakefield and his colleagues 'collected as many old clothes as we could and proceeded to dress up the imposing statue outside the Grand, hoping the whole Oxford team would be arrested for the outrage.' Unluckily for them, the law was alive to the plot, and Cambridge took to its collective heels in flight. With a body swerve here, and an outside break or two there, they outstripped their uniformed pursuers, but it was a different matter when it came to the Varsity Match. As if impressed by the fleetness of their backs in eluding the police, the Cambridge forwards consistently laid the ball back instead of driving through the weaker Oxford pack. Failing to see the error of their ways, and persisting with a game plan that wasn't working, they were well beaten, 11–5.

The following month, Wakefield was back in England colours as they travelled to Cardiff as reigning champions to open their new international season. The pitch was 'a squelching morass', on which, the visitors complained, it was difficult to stand up and football was virtually impossible. Possibly, but the Welsh managed to solve the problem by having, according to Wakefield, 'phenomenally long studs, longer indeed than I have ever seen, and I imagine they had considerably outgrown the regulation size.' Wakefield could think as he pleased, but the fact remained that one side played intelligent and effective rugby, well suited to the conditions, and the other did not. Consequently the game, reported Colonel Philip Trevor the next day, 'was one long, unbroken series of victories for the Welsh forwards, whereas the England back division never looked like atoning for the sins of their forwards, who were routed although they were half a stone per man heavier.' Wales won 28–6. Lesson number two for Wakefield, who conceded that the match was a fiasco, and that 'on such a day, the extremely clever cross-dribbling of the Welsh pack was of a kind that should be used more in modern football.'

Despite being up at Cambridge, Wakefield was also captain of the strong RAF side. In those days, the Services teams played a full list of fixtures against the leading clubs, building towards the well-publicised climax of the inter-services tournament, which the RAF was tipped to win. The game against the Navy was a tight affair, decided by a single score. Wakefield thought he was the one to get it as he crossed the line but, before he could touch down, he had the mortification of having the ball knocked out of his hands, giving victory to the Navy. Ah, well, there was always the Army game, in which the RAF's strong forwards appeared to be well on top as the match unfolded. Despite being a forward, Wakefield was fast and, as captain, took the fateful decision to come out of the scrum and into the three-quarter line. This sounds a strange tactic to modern ears, but not unusual in the early years of the century when there were as many arguments in favour of seven forwards and eight backs as vice versa. But on this occasion, it all went horribly wrong. With the extra man up front, the Army took control of the scrum, denied the RAF possession of the ball, and ran out easy winners. Painful lesson number three for Wakefield.

To cap it all, Wakefield had passed up the Varsity 100 yards finals to play in the Services match. Otherwise, he'd have been running against Harold Abrahams and, who knows, with a small twist of fate it might have been Wakefield, not Abrahams, competing at the 1924 Olympics and going on to become the legend of *Chariots of Fire!*

World Champs For 91 Years – and Still Counting

France v United States of America, Olympic Games, Paris, May 1924

Rugby was one of the earliest sports to be included in the Olympics, in 1900, and although they were still a decade away from contesting the Five Nations, France lifted gold by beating Germany, and Great Britain took bronze. A medal, of whatever colour, came as a surprise to the motley crew of British players, who had thought they were playing in an exhibition match as a sideshow of the concurrent Paris Universal Exhibition. Whether or not they were miffed at winning only bronze, the home unions elected to regard the Olympics as a showpiece event for emerging countries, and henceforth had nothing to do with them, accidentally or otherwise.

In the 1920 Antwerp Games, France were silver medallists, but as the sport attracted even fewer entrants than in 1900, to wit two, this was not an achievement to cause flutterings in, say, Auckland or Johannesburg, especially as their conquerors were the USA. By 1924, the competing countries had increased by fifty per cent, requiring France to beat Romania (61–3) in the semi-final or the first round, depending on your viewpoint, before confronting the Americans again at the Stade Colombes in Paris. France were at full Five Nations strength, but the ferocity of American tackling saw them retain the gold medal by 17–3 in front of a crowd that was, not to put too fine a point on it, rowdily partisan.

'If the team representing the Stars and Stripes is going to be hissed every time it wins an Olympic title, it would be better to return home and concern ourselves no longer with international athletics,' was the typical view of one American pressman. Just as well George W Bush wasn't president then, or there'd have been a gunboat up the Seine before you could say Donald Rumsfeld. French pride was sufficiently dented for an official enquiry into whether the

Americans had fielded professional gridiron players, but their boys were genuine Union fellers from Stanford University and so, with much muttering, the French had to put up with silver. Rugby then disappeared from the Olympic menu, leaving the USA as champions. They have yet to be dispossessed.

Don't Worry, I'll Probably Get One Over in the End

South Africa v British & Irish Lions, Port Elizabeth, third Test, September 1924

Every kicker has the odd off day, and sometimes a kind of immortality is assured if a potentially match-winning kick in front of the posts misses its target. Ask Gavin Hastings (see page 51). But to miss every kick in an entire series is something else again.

The British Isles team that Ronnie Cove-Smith captained in South Africa was the first to be nicknamed the Lions, but they scarcely raised a growl in the four-Test series. They suffered horribly from injuries, starting on the outward voyage. Jamie Clinch, an enthusiastic thespian, was entertainments officer for the journey, and vastly amused his team-mates by jarring his spine so badly while performing in a revue he'd written and directed that he was ruled out of the early games. Of the three fullbacks, one was injured in the first practice game and the second in the first tour match, leaving Dan Drysdale – luckily a player of resource and panache, if not an outstanding kicker – to soldier on alone in that position. The tour was a constant struggle to cobble together fifteen players fit enough to turn out in any position. Drysdale had to play in virtually every game.

In terms of Tests, the series was a disaster, with three lost and one drawn, and if the series is memorable at all, it is for two reasons. On the Springbok side it marked the international debut of their remarkable fly-half Bennie Osier, who was to revolutionise the use of tactical kicking from that position and, in his later years, form a superlative half-back combination with Danie Craven. On the Lions' side, poor Dan Drysdale achieved unwelcome notoriety by missing every kick at goal that came his way. Starting as he meant to go on, he missed a straightforward conversion in the first Test, which the Springboks won 7–3, but the real clanger came in the third. On a miserable windy day, the South Africans just could not get their game together, and with the score 3–3, Drysdale had a penalty bang in front, and missed that as well. He was an outstanding player, who won 26 caps for Scotland, and deserves better than to be remembered for his failure with the boot.

What Me, Ref?
You Cannot Be Serious!
England v New Zealand, Twickenham, January 1925

In these days of punch-ups and sin bins, being sent off is no longer the shameful event that it was in 1925 when All Black second-row Cyril Brownlie was given his marching orders in the opening minutes of the match against England. He ensured his name would be remembered not only as the first player to be dismissed in an international but, for many years, the only one. But what had the poor chap done? A kind of *omertà* seemed to fall over Twickenham and, to this day, no-one really knows.

We do know that England kicked off and immediately a loose maul developed in which, both New Zealand and English accounts agree, 'play became overzealous and the referee issued a general warning to the forwards.' To put it plainly, a first-class brawl developed, and four players were warned, two from each side. Three minutes later, referee Albert Freethy blew again and, it is said, warned both packs that the next offending player would be testing the temperature of the showers earlier than planned. Almost immediately after the restart, Brownlie was singled out for the privilege. The ubiquitous Colonel Philip Trevor announced to a waiting world that Mr Freethy had seen him 'deliberately kick a player lying on the ground'.

Maybe, but no-one in the vicinity would come clean about what had happened. Len Corbett, the England centre, admitted that 'robust forward play was the feature of the opening phases', but defended Brownlie as a 'magnificent forward', and Mr Freethy as 'the ablest, firmest and fairest referee'. Splendid.

So what happened? Wavell Wakefield gave an oblique clue, stemming from the All Black formation of a two-man front row. 'Instead of packing in the centre of our three-man front row, which naturally would always have given us the loose head, they kept trying to work the loose head for themselves.' Reg Edwards, the England prop, wasn't going to have that. We can only guess that Edwards' determination to let the All Blacks get away with nothing led to a private war in which Brownlie's were the last set of fingerprints. It did England no good. They lost 17–11, and Cyril's brother, Maurice, redeemed the family honour by scoring New Zealand's third try.

The French Have a Cunning Plan

Scotland v France, Inverleith, February 1925

Having disposed of every team they met in the British Isles, the 1925 All Blacks marched on to Paris and destroyed France 30–6. This was during the prolonged period in which New Zealand played with seven forwards and seven backs, using the fifteenth player as a combination flanker-cum-scrum-half, linking forwards and three-quarters. The French were much impressed with this, and for their first match of the home nations series, away against Scotland, decided they'd catch the Scots off guard by playing All Black style. Wing forward Bioussa was therefore instructed to withdraw from the pack and make himself useful in other parts of the field.

This was an immensely cunning wheeze, but one that contained a number of disadvantages that, in their excitement, the French had forgotten to think through. The first was that Scotland, while having a fast and exciting set of backs, were worried that their lightweight scrum might not contain the opposition, and they were accordingly delighted to find that their eight forwards had to contend with only seven opponents who, unlike the All Blacks, had not been picked for strength nor trained to play the seven-man game. Nor had the French given much thought to what poor old Bioussa might do when banished from the safe world of the scrum to the very public glare of life in the open spaces behind it. He seems to have spent the afternoon floating around haphazardly, bumping into his colleagues and causing Gallic consternation all round.

All of this provided Scotland with one of their happiest afternoons, and Ian Smith on the left wing with four tries, in a 25–4 romp to victory. Gifted such a wonderful start to their campaign, Scotland marched on to Cardiff, where Ian Smith ran in another four tries, and carried on to achieve their first-ever Grand Slam. France went through the series losing every game, as they had in 1924 and were to do again in 1926.

Time to Give Up

Wales v Scotland, Cardiff; England v Wales, Twickenham, 1931

When they met in 1931 Wales beat Scotland 13–8 in a game unremarkable except for one curious and unique fact – Wales scored most of their points before or after normal time. For reasons that passed without comment at the time, the referee signalled the kickoff three minutes before the scheduled moment. Wales won possession and the ball went out to J C Morley on the wing. Although not particularly fast, Morley had a good body swerve and an excellent change of pace, and broke through to touch down in less than two minutes.

Scotland's fightback levelled the score at eight points all by normal full-time. The concept of adding time on for injuries did exist then, but was somewhat haphazardly applied, if at all, at the referee's whim. On this occasion, play ran on for a couple of minutes, which, as it transpired, was all Wales needed. The ball went down the line to Ronnie Boon, on the opposite wing to Morley. It was a poor pass and he knocked on but the referee, possibly dreaming of his approaching cup of tea, ignored the infringement. Boon kicked the ball over the line and won the sprint to touch down.

Another statistical curiosity, given the rarity of drawn internationals, is that in the decade 1926 to 1936, England and Wales drew four times. At Twickenham in 1931 was the second of those occasions and, again, owed something to the referee, Ireland's Dr J R Wheeler. Bristol and England centre Don Burland attempted the conversion of his own try, which had levelled the score at 6–6. The ball shaved the post, but the touch judges could not agree on which side. The referee appeared to signal a miss, and the scoreboard remained unchanged. At the interval, Dr Wheeler looked up at the board and raised eight fingers. To rejoicing among the home fans, the England score increased by two while the lads in white were engaged in nothing more strenuous than sucking their half-time oranges. England earned an 11–11 draw with practically the last kick of the game and gained their only point of the season. Wales were champions, but that lost point cost them the Triple Crown and Grand Slam.

Just a Kick Away From Disaster

Horrendous tales of missed conversions, 1932, 1962 & 1991

'The greatest conversion since St Paul,' the Welsh called John Taylor's miracle kick from a muddy touchline that gave Wales victory by a point over Scotland in 1971 (see page 78) and led them on to the Grand Slam. For every wonder kick there has probably been an equally glaring cockup from in front of the posts. Some are quickly erased from the memory, but others are the difference between victory and defeat.

Between the wars, Ireland rarely did well in Cardiff, and when they arrived there for the very last match of the 1932 season it was to face a Welsh side for whom victory meant the Triple Crown and the championship. Irish sides were famous throughout much of the century for their fire in the first three-quarters of the game and their lack of puff in the last, and Cardiff 1932 was no exception to the rule. Ireland were leading 12–7 as the game entered its final sixty seconds, when Welsh fly-half Ray Ralph 'raced through a scattered [i.e. exhausted] defence to score near the posts'. Up stepped skipper and fullback Jack Bassett for the easy conversion that would give Wales the championship outright. But poor Jack Bassett had made two mistakes to let in half of Ireland's four tries, and may not have been feeling as chipper as usual. He missed. Ireland won 12–10 and shared the championship, and Wales would wait until 1950 for the Triple Crown. Bassett never played for them again.

A Welsh fullback was the victim of repeated misfortune of a similar nature thirty years later, this time at Twickenham where, in those days when one end of the ground was open, the swirling wind was tricky for those who had not encountered it before. The finger of fate in the England–Wales game of 1962 was pointing at Kevin Coslett, winning his first cap. Even in club games, he was noted for preparing his kicks with an attention to detail that Dave Aldred, later to be the kicking guru of the professional era, would thoroughly approve, so the five penalty opportunities that came his way against England demanded extra-special care. They were not all simple, short-range pots, to be sure, but as each penalty came and, scoreless, went again, the time he took to map out the ground, judge the wind and polish his kicking toe got longer and longer. By the time of his fifth and final attempt, with the crowd yet to be roused from the languor of a scoreless encounter, he seemed almost afraid to kick at all. It took him 75 seconds, and still he sent it the wrong side of the posts. At the end of the game, the stewards woke the crowd up to inform them the match had finished 0–0, and they were free to go. The authorities decreed that, in the interests of some kind of movement on the pitch, sixty seconds would be the maximum allowed for future kicks.

England had swept to the Grand Slam in 1991, but seemed strangely unsure of themselves in the World Cup that same summer. They reached the semi-final and found themselves facing Scotland back at Murrayfield, scene of their humiliation in 1990 (see page 114). Scotland had gone ahead 6–0 with penalties from Gavin Hastings, who had had a magnificent tournament with the boot, and England had dragged themselves level with two Jon Webb kicks when, as the last quarter began, Scotland were given a penalty virtually straight in front of England's posts from point-blank range. The reliable Gavin stepped up – and shot it to the right of the posts. 'None of us could quite believe it,' said brother Scott, 'and I don't think Gavin could either.' To compound his misery, Rob Andrew dropped a goal ten minutes later and England went through to the final, 9–6.

By an extraordinary statistical quirk, the score and the scorers were exactly the same as in the Calcutta Cup match three years before. On that occasion, Hastings had landed two penalties, Webb had replied in kind to level the scores, and Andrew had sealed things with a drop kick. But the World Cup is an altogether different proposition than the Calcutta Cup, and there had been no dramatic penalty miss. Keeping a commendable sense of proportion, Gavin said after the semi-final disaster: 'It would have changed the game, but I can live with it. There are more important things in life.' But then, other than dashing off to compose a suicide note, what else can one say?

Sic Transit Gloria Mundi

England v Wales, Twickenham, January 1933

One would have thought that Ronnie Boon would live long in Welsh folk memory after scoring the drop goal and the try that gave Wales victory by seven points to three over England. It was, after all, their only victory of the season and, more significantly, the first-ever win at Twickenham in almost a quarter of a century of trying.

The game itself was ordinary. In an echo of things to come later in the century, *The Times* correspondent took the respective fly-halves to task for failing to get their three-quarters moving: 'The centres ... were scarcely given one helpful pass. The best of Elliot and Bowcott's runs had no more than personal value. One refuses to believe that this was enough.' Only two events stuck in the memory. To begin with, did Elliot score a try to open the scoring for England? According to the record book, he did. As he dived for the line, he was tackled heavily and the ball appeared to jerk forward before he could touch down. Not even Elliot himself was convinced it was a valid score. In the second half Boon, on the Welsh right wing, who was moving regularly infield to escape the close marking, dropped a goal to put Wales into the lead, 4–3. With ten minutes to go, and England down to fourteen men, he also scored Wales's try, to make it 7–3. The conversion attempt by Vivien Jenkins sailed at least a foot wide of the right-hand post. The Welsh touch judge raised his flag triumphantly. His English counterpart kept his firmly by his side, and the referee did not whistle. Nevertheless, the scoreboard showed 9–3, which, so far as the crowd was concerned, meant that England needed two scores, not one, to save the game.

Many years later, Cliff Morgan, the great Wales and Lions fly-half of the 1950s, later head of the BBC's Outside Broadcasts, was participating in a sports forum. A man in the audience asked the panel who had scored the winning Welsh try at Twickenham in 1933. After several unsuccessful guesses, the panel gave up. 'I bloody did,' said the questioner (or so, at least, the story goes) and Ronnie Boon left the room.

Never Mind His Leg, Man, Go For His Finger

New Zealand v South Africa, Auckland, September 1937

Between the two world wars, indeed until apartheid raised its ugly barrier, Springboks and Kiwis were convinced that world rugby supremacy was a matter to be decided only among themselves, and their tussles were not for the faint-hearted. Prior to South Africa's tour of New Zealand in 1937, their meetings had always finished on level terms and, running true to history, this series stood at one apiece as 55,000 spectators gathered at Eden Park for the third and final Test.

Winning his sixth cap for the All Blacks was 'Brushey' Mitchell, a born humorist and a strong, pacey back who sometimes played in the centre, but was reckoned to be better on the wing, from which position he'd put in some good performances on the All Blacks' 1935–6 tour of Britain. Brushey had been carrying a leg injury and had missed the first two South African Tests but, after a run-out in heavy strapping, the selectors seemed determined to have him for the decider. This was where the mistakes began. Jack Sullivan had been New Zealand's outstanding centre in the first two encounters, so he was moved to the wing for the third Test. Mitchell, the only one with international experience on the wing, was moved into the centre to replace him. All perfectly logical so far?

Whatever the state of Mitchell's leg, it was another part of his anatomy that proved the weak link. Louis Brabow, the 22-year-old Springbok centre down to play opposite Brushey, went with his coach to watch the Blacks at practice two days before the match. 'We noticed that the All Black star centre, brought in especially for this match, had a strapped finger which caused him to wince when he caught the ball or had to tackle someone. We decided to try breaks at centre from the start of the game. Brushey Mitchell just could not cope, and we burst past him time and again.'

The Springboks ran in five tries that day, Brabow getting a couple of them, and beat New Zealand 17–6. It was not until 1956 that the All Blacks finally won a series against South Africa. As Brabow said, 'Do not play an injured player, no matter how famous.'

A Clear Case of
Moving the Goalposts

England v Scotland, Twickenham, March 1938

It's all there on television – or would be, had all the archive film survived – to show us how Hal Sever, with a few minutes left, the line at his mercy, the ball in his hands and the winning score beckoning, managed to run into the post and lose the match for England. It's become one of the great stories of rugby folklore, but did it really happen like that?

The Calcutta Cup clash of 1938, played for the Triple Crown and the championship, and the first international to be televised, was an epic encounter. 'I cannot remember a more interesting and remarkable match,' wrote Howard Marshall about Scotland's dramatic 21–16 victory, 'and I am quite prepared to swallow my national pride and welcome the fact that attack beat defence so decisively.' England played the first half with a strong wind behind them yet failed to take advantage, scoring only one try, and landing two penalties, in response to Scotland's four tries. With the wind behind them in the second half, everyone expected Scotland to run riot, but it was England, monopolising the ball in the tight, who did most of the pressing. 'The England forwards did enough to win the match four times over,' Marshall reckoned. 'If they had kept the ball, they probably *would* have won it.' As it was, they repeatedly gave it to their backs, and their backs were repeatedly run down by the Scottish flankers. The Scots three-quarters, on the other hand, were 'so swift, so intelligent and beautiful that I almost wished they had the English forwards to give them the ball.' Stalemate threatened. A penalty and a drop goal from England, answered by two penalties from Scotland meant that, with under ten minutes remaining, Scotland were clinging to a narrow 18–16 lead. England's attacks became ever more desperate as they hunted a score that would give them the lead and the Triple Crown.

Hal Sever was one of the outstanding English three-quarters of the 1930s. When Obolensky scored his two tries in the historic 13–0 victory over the 1936 All Blacks, Sever ran 35 yards to score England's third. In 1937, he scored what the *Telegraph* called 'the try of a lifetime' against Ireland, running 60 yards for the 'sort of try which the hero of a school story scores in the last chapter', to give England a one-point victory. These were not the least of his exploits, and Hal Sever was a man who knew exactly where the line was, and how to get there.

Now, against the Scots, Peter Cranmer had punted ahead, England had gathered the ball and worked it down the line to Sever who cut in to touch down under the post – and ran into it! The ball went loose, Scotland swept upfield, and Wilson Shaw scored the dramatic try, immortalised on old film, that clinched the last Calcutta Cup match before World War II. That's the legend, and it's perfectly true it was Scotland, not England, who got the winning score on the stroke of time. But Sever's party with the woodwork was not at the time reported as the later story has it, nor is it how Sever himself remembered it in his still-vigorous nineties. Yes, he did cut in towards the line to touch down between the posts, but he had at least three Scots closing on him and, as one tackled him from behind, another drove into him from the side, forcing him up against the post. Howard Marshall, indeed, described him as being 'pulled down inches short by four desperate Scotsmen'. But it makes for a wonderful legend, and one Sever continued to chuckle over, despite the slur on his reputation.

The woodwork had not entirely finished leaping into the path of the English, but next time it changed sides. Fifty-five years later, England – and fullback Jonathan Webb in particular – were having a torrid time playing France at Twickenham in a blustering wind. They had already conceded two tries when, late in the first half, they struck gold – or at least the crossbar – from a Webb penalty attempt. The ball rebounded perfectly into the arms of Ian Hunter, following up at full gallop, who scored the only try England had looked like getting. With France trailing 15–16, and only minutes left to play, first Didier Cambarabero, then Aubin Hueber, tried to drop a goal, and on each occasion the ball hit the crossbar and fell back on the French side.

Cup Suckers

**Guy's v St Mary's, 1949; Penclawdd v Newport, 1980;
Bath v Waterloo, 1992; Cardiff v St Peter's, 1993**

Not so long ago in time, but a world away in attitudes, the annual Hospitals Cup was a highlight of the rugby season. Medical centres, especially the big teaching hospitals, were, after all, teeming with middle-class young men, incarcerated for six long years of study, who had the advantage of being able to patch up the eye they'd just gouged or put back the shoulder they'd just dislocated. The 1949 Cup Final between Guy's and St Mary's was a desperately close affair. Guy's had one hand on the trophy when they converted a try late in the second half to take a 5–3 lead. In a last desperate rush, St Mary's were awarded a penalty from way out on the touchline, with a stiff breeze blowing against the kicker. While Guy's strung themselves out thinly along the goal line, St Mary's fullback, Beatson, who may have fancied himself in amateur dramatics, made deceptively elaborate preparations to take the kick. Suddenly he tapped the ball forward, caught it and went for the line like a homing pigeon, touching down for a try, which the referee awarded.

St Mary's lifted the Cup, but Beatson's score caused great controversy. Did it contravene Law 24, as it then was? Had he indicated a kick at goal and therefore forfeited the right to take a tap penalty? Many believed that, if Guy's had appealed formally, the referee might have been forced to reverse his ruling.

Moving towards more recent times, you won't want to be reminded of the name Penclawdd if you come from Newport (and you might struggle to pronounce it if you come from anywhere else). By 1980, Newport were no longer able to boast quite the pedigree they had carried for much of the twentieth century, but they were still one of the leading Welsh club sides. So a trip to the P-place for a Cup tie seemed a routine affair for them, even if the wet and windy conditions made the fixture something to be got through as quickly as possible. Penclawdd had had its moment of past glory. In the 1930s Haydn Tanner and Willie Davis, one of the great Welsh half-back combinations, had come from there. Now, the roll of honour was about to add another name – Kevin Dallimore, their open-side flanker. He charged down a clearance kick from Newport's Keith James, hunted the ball down and scored in the corner. In the appalling conditions, Penclawdd out-tussled their distinguished opponents and hung on to win 4–0.

Over the border in England, twelve years later, Bath travelled to Liverpool for a Pilkington Cup tie against Waterloo who, though once the home of England No 8 Alan Ashcroft, were no longer a force to be reckoned with – or so Bath thought, as they gave Stuart Barnes and Ben Clarke leave to go and play for the Barbarians. Their strength reduced to a mere eleven full internationals, Bath were not to know that the opposition contained a future star, albeit one who would switch to Northampton before gaining England honours, Paul Grayson. His three penalties outdid Bath's penalty and try and, with Jerry Guscott unaccountably squandering a four-to-two overlap in favour of an unsuccessful drop-goal attempt, Bath had to pack their Pilkington bags for 1992.

Just one year later, both Newport and Bath had cause to thank Cardiff as their cup clanger erased the memory of all that had gone before. On hearing they had been drawn at home against fourth division St Peter's, Cardiff, the great name of Welsh club rugby as the century approached its end, made an extra space on their scoreboard to accommodate a three-figure score. Just as well to be prepared, boyo. With an eye to future demands, they also elected to rest half the first XV so that they would be fresh for the following league game. There's forward planning for you. When Goliath went into his home fixture with David he made the same mistake as Cardiff in not checking first to see if the opposition had any surprise weaponry up its shirt. St Peter's aptly named winger Gareth Snook cocked his appellation at Cardiff as he scored an unconverted try in the first half, and stand-off Alun Edwards landed three penalties as St Peter's won 16–14, to the joy of most people except Cardiff's Aussie coach, Alec Evans. The referee, he claimed in one of the season's least gracious comments in defeat, was 'a five-dollar official in a \$20,000 competition'. The St Peter's coach, former Cardiff player Lawrence O'Brien, just pointed at the scoreboard and said simply: 'They underestimated us.' And how!

To Lose Once in a Day is Unfortunate, But Twice is Careless

South Africa v New Zealand; Australia v New Zealand; September 1949

It's unlikely anyone in New Zealand rugby circles saw the tenth anniversary of the outbreak of World War II, 3 September 1949, as a dire portent, but it proved to be the blackest day of the blackest year in the Blacks' history. When the powers that be drew up the schedule of international matches for that year, they agreed to a tour of South Africa, with four Tests, running in parallel with a two-Test series against Australia for the Bledisloe Cup. To be sure, the Springboks had not played an international since 1938, whereas the Blacks had played four Tests since peace was declared, all against Australia, and won the lot; nor had the Australians managed to wrench the Bledisloe from New Zealand's possessive embrace since 1934. Even so, in retrospect it seems an extraordinary act of hubris to send your thirty best players to South Africa while simultaneously putting out an effective third XV to defend the Bledisloe, even if it did contain three players – centre Johnny Smith, fly-half Ben Couch and scrum-half Vince Bevan – who would probably have been in South Africa but for the fact that, as Maoris, they were debarred from that country on racial grounds.

The first game to kick off on this 'extraordinary day of humiliation', as one press comment put it, was the first Test against Australia in Wellington. Wallaby forwards have never been a soft touch and it was up front, especially in the lineout, that New Zealand lost the match. Australia scored three tries in the first half, two of them the direct result of poor lineout work exploited by wing Ralph Garner and flanker Colin Windon. Garner scored again just before half-time when the Kiwi fullback, Rex Orr, came into the line and dropped the ball, enabling Australia to kick into the space left vacant and Garner to run onto the ball and score. Apart from a second-half penalty, the

All Blacks had to wait until the last minute of the match to score a try in the corner after one of their rare backline movements. Australia's 11–6 victory was their first over New Zealand for fifteen years. Nine of the All Black team were dropped, never playing for their country again, but three weeks later the Wallabies won again, this time by 16–9, and took the Bledisloe Cup back home to Oz.

As the sun moved westwards on 3 September, the All Blacks' second international match of the day prepared to get under way in Durban. After the epic struggles between the Blacks and the Springboks in the first third of the century, South Africa had finally broken the deadlock by two matches to one in 1937. Twelve years later, rugby supremacy was at stake, but the All Blacks were already 2–0 down in the series and a crisis was at hand. Skipper and centre Fred 'Needle' Allen, although destined to become one of the greatest of All Black coaches, overseeing a run of 37 consecutive unbeaten games between 1966 and 1969, was dropped. In the front row, 20-year-old prop Kevin Skinner was on a learning curve that would see his toughness become the stuff of legends. 'I weighed about fourteen stone five then and I was packing down against these big South Africans [Chris Koch and Okey Geffin] who were all sixteen stone and more. Hell, at the end of it I had a neck like a bloody ox!'

Within seven minutes, the All Blacks were 6–0 down through two penalties kicked by prop Geffin, the regular Springbok place kicker. From then on, the New Zealand pack gained the upper hand and exerted a dominance the Springboks couldn't break. The problem was their inability to convert this into any other score than a single try midway through the first half from centre Morrie Goddard after the Springbok fullback Jack van der Schyff (see page 64) was caught in possession. Otherwise, the South African defence proved rock solid, and when Geffin kicked a third penalty three minutes into the second half the scoring was over, and New Zealand lost a game they probably deserved to win, by 9–3. It was small consolation to them that, for the second time in three Tests, South Africa had had to rely on penalties to win – indeed in the four Tests of the series, the Springboks scored only three tries. A fortnight later, the All Blacks lost the final Test 11–8 in a humiliating whitewash.

The Long Drought That Followed a 44-Point Downpour

Scotland v South Africa, Murrayfield, November 1951

The year 1951 had dawned with such promise for the Scots. In February, the largest crowd then seen at an international rugby match, 80,000, had witnessed a thrilling and unexpected 19–0 victory at Murrayfield over a Welsh side full of British Lions. To be sure, these were the only two points Scotland won in that year's championship, but the magnificent spoiling play of flanker Doug Elliott and the exciting running of their young backs gave promise of great things in the future. What no-one foresaw was the effect that the mighty Springbok rugby machine would have when it rumbled north to Edinburgh on 24 November that year, to meet a Scottish team that had been selected without a trial game, and whose pre-match preparation consisted of a run round the pitch on Friday afternoon.

'Surely,' wrote E W Swanton of their 44–0 victory, 'the Springboks have never won a game, against opponents of international class so brilliantly and conclusively.' By the second half, it was reported, Scotland looked slow, inept, unwilling to tackle and in the grip of paralysing despair. Under the modern scoring system, the Springboks' nine tries, seven conversions and one drop goal would have counted 62 points, and it was the biggest international try count since the ten South Africa had scored against Ireland in 1912, two world wars earlier. Their ruthless player, manager and administrator, Danie Craven, said, 'We shouldn't have done that to them. We took away their pride, and left them with nothing.' Scotland's hooker, Norman Mair, who missed the Springbok game, confirmed his sentiment when he later wrote: 'It was one of those awful days when everything went wrong. It had the same effect as an air crash might have if it had involved the whole national team.'

What followed was a run of seventeen consecutive defeats in which Scotland registered just 53 points, an average of barely three a game, and it was to be four years before they rediscovered the taste of victory as captain and fullback Angus Cameron led them to a 14–8 win over Wales. Small wonder that, north of the border, 24 November 1951 is still remembered as 'The Blackest Day'.

Crocodiles Only Eat You

South Africa v British & Irish Lions, Johannesburg, August 1955

When Johnny Hammond's victorious British Isles team returned from South Africa in 1896 it wouldn't have crossed their minds that they would be in their eighties before another British team so much as avoided defeat in a Test rubber there. The 90,000 crowd that swarmed into the ground for the first Test of the Lions' 1955 visit was therefore confident of seeing the high priests of Springbok rugby sacrifice fifteen Lions to their national religion. Recalled to fullback for the Springboks, after a six-year gap, Jack van der Schyff was seeking atonement. Against the All Blacks in 1949 he had kicked so badly that his duties were taken over by a prop, and since props in those days would have regarded a carthorse as a dainty mover, public humiliation couldn't sink much lower. Or could it?

The Lions' brilliant back line, including Cliff Morgan and Jeff Butterfield, ran in five tries against the Springboks' four, two of them coming courtesy of van der Schyff. Twice he failed to field high balls letting in first Jeff Greenwood, then Tony O'Reilly, for tries. But early in the second half, injury reduced the Lions to fourteen men and, although they looked impregnable at 23–11 with less than twenty minutes to go, the extra workload and the effect of playing at altitude began to take its toll. The Springboks threw everything at them and with two tries brought the score back to 23–19 as the game reached the third minute of injury time. In a last, surging effort, winger Theunis Briers crossed the line to make it 23–22 with only the formality of the conversion to come. As van der Schyff placed the ball midway between touchline and posts, the scorers took down the figure 2, ready to replace it with a 4 to signal a 24–23 victory. Schyff lifted his head and hooked the ball wide of the left-hand post. Predictably, he was vilified from one end of the country to the other, but there is a happy ending of sorts. The Lions drew the rubber 2–2, and Schyff left the country to take up hunting, finding gentler companions among the crocodiles of the Rhodesian (now Zimbabwean) bush.

Aussie Nerve Cracks at the Death – Twice

Ireland v Australia, England v Australia, January/February 1958

Many rugby matches are settled in the closing minutes and a last-gasp defeat can happen to anyone, but to suffer the same fate twice, in successive Tests, flirts with carelessness. Not within living memory had Ireland won a Test against a visiting southern hemisphere side. When the Wallabies came to Lansdowne Road, few of the multitudes gathered in the Dublin bars before kickoff expected any kind of contest, let alone a victory for the boys in green.

With seven minutes to go Ireland, playing into a half-gale and, as usual, running out of steam in the last quarter, were 6–3 down when, amazingly, they levelled the score with an unconverted try. Even so, to dream of victory was to believe in leprechaun's gold – and yet, within five minutes, Ireland intercepted a wild Wallaby pass on the halfway line, and centre Noel Henderson set off gamely for the try line. Any other three-quarter would have been in under the posts with time to order a Guinness but Henderson, amply built, was not a flyer and with the crowd holding its breath, he lumbered ever onwards. He was caught a yard from the line 'but the tackler glanced off,' reported Michael Melford, 'like a destroyer off a battleship, and he fell over the line amid a din which must have echoed from Kerry to Donegal' to give Ireland a famous 9–6 victory.

If the Australians were disappointed by their failure to close the game out in Dublin, they were devastated a fortnight later when, at Twickenham, lightning struck in near-identical fashion. In 'one of the hardest and most exciting games ever seen at Twickenham, played at frenetic pace', England lost fly-half Phil Horrocks-Taylor early in the first half and were condemned to play with fourteen men. Twice behind to a penalty and a dropped goal, they twice pulled level with a try and a penalty, and the match was coming up to full-time when winger Peter Jackson completed one last English surge 'with a weaving, feinting run before he threw himself over in the extreme right corner'. The Wallabies had missed no less than three tackles on Jackson as, once again, they lost 9–6.

Rum Goings-on at Ellis Park

South Africa v France, second Test, Johannesburg, August 1958

After a match against Ireland in freezing temperatures, David Marques – who, with John Currie, formed a powerful second row for England in the late 1950s – was asked how he coped with the cold. He explained that 'the wave of alcohol that came from the Irish pack anaesthetised you against it'. The cold could hardly account for Lucien Mias, the inspirational forward and captain of the French team touring South Africa in 1958, putting away half a bottle of rum during the interval of the second Test against the Springboks. A simpler conclusion is that he played well on the stuff.

In 1952, France had been badly beaten in Paris by the South Africans. Mias was in the French side, took the humiliation badly and, with Jean Prat ('Monsieur Rugby'), set about rebuilding French rugby. In 1954, France shared the Five Nations title and beat the visiting All Blacks, so the rehabilitation was in progress when Mias decided to take four years out to complete his medical studies. Now he was back.

The first Test against the Springboks at Newlands had been a drab 3–3 draw, and it preceded a thorough French stuffing inflicted by a scratch provincial combination. It was the best thing that could have happened. Periodically, the South Africans have indulged the fantasy that their forwards are invincible.

Now they were sure of it and, off guard, they lost both the forward battle and the tactical encounter in the second Test. Two dropped goals and a penalty gave France a 9–5 victory. It was the first time the Springboks had lost a home series in sixty years.

'The South Africans thought we were a second-class team,' Mias was to write and added, foreshadowing the Lions' famous 'ninety-nine' battle cry sixteen years in the future, 'and from time to time we had to prove and demonstrate that we had both physical strength and spirit.' If the Springbok reaction was one of the deepest gloom, the joy of the French was unconfined. In the dressing room the tears of joy flowed freely and the effect on the French public was electric. Rugby was elevated to a new level, and the following season France were outright Five Nations champions for the first time in their history. Mias's bottle of rum packed a powerful punch.

Can You Kick It From Here If I Blow For a Penalty?

New Zealand v British & Irish Lions, Dunedin, July 1959

Even in the days of phenomenally accurate place kickers like Naas Botha, Neil Jenkins, Andrew Mehrtens and Jonny Wilkinson, the name of All Black Don Clarke remains a byword for reliability. No matter the range or the angle, if Clarke was taking aim against you, it was probable the points would click up on the board. It's a shame, therefore, that his reputation has been overshadowed, at least in British and South African eyes, by the doubtful refereeing that gave him the chance to tee up some of his successful efforts.

South Africa had left New Zealand in 1956 upset by the standard of refereeing. When they lost 9–6 to Canterbury after a bitterly disputed penalty, their manager Danie Craven had taken the unusual step of lodging an official complaint, and their temper had not been improved by Don Clarke's eight points from the boot in their 11–5 loss to the Kiwis in the final Test.

Three years later, the Lions squared up to the All Blacks in the first Test and played sparkling rugby to win the try count 4–0. Nevertheless, they lost the match 18–17 as Allan Fleury, the local referee, awarded the All Blacks fourteen penalties, six within Don Clarke's range and three of them within the last ten minutes of the game when the Lions were ahead 17–9. 'Never before in representative rugby has a side been so outplayed in all departments except goal-kicking, and won despite the fact that the opposition scored four tries,' was typical of the views of the assembled press corps. 'The Lions were bewildered with many of Mr Fleury's decisions, particularly those in the closing minutes which changed the whole course of the match.' A prominent Kiwi journalist wrote: 'The crowd in its shame called for the Lions to win.'

Thereafter, the tour continued on a wave of goodwill. The Lions lost the rubber 3–1 but, when they won the final Test, the crowd spontaneously broke into 'Now is the Hour', the Maori song of farewell. The debate started by this game led to the value of the try being upgraded to four points twelve years later.

A Cure for Insomnia

Scotland v Wales, Murrayfield,
February 1963

If, gentle reader, you are under the age of sixty or so you can count yourself fortunate to have no memory of the day Wales travelled to Murrayfield in search of their first win there for ten years. Should you, on the other hand, be slippered and white-bearded and given to fond reminiscence of matches past, the memory of this meeting – contest being too strong a word – will still make you beg for release from the nightmare. It was the year of the great freeze, one of the worst winters on record, and the muffled spectators in the stands and on the terraces must have been tempted to imitate Captain Oates, and slip outside for a few moments to embrace a frozen death, rather than endure the tedium for which they had unwittingly parted with good money. This must surely have been the most boring game of international rugby ever played.

Welsh rugby had much for which to thank Clive Rowlands, who played fourteen games at scrum-half, all of them as captain, and was instrumental in opening the door to the Welsh glory years that lay ahead. At Murrayfield in 1963, though, rugby in general had nothing to thank him for except, as a result of his tactics that day, a change in the law that came soon after. In those dear, distant days, the laws permitted you to kick into touch from any position on the field and retain the put-in, a ruling that Osier and Craven had exploited in the 1930s on behalf of the Springboks. Here, at Murrayfield, Rowlands was even more ruthless in exposing the absurdity of the law. Boot the ball into touch, lineout, back to Rowlands, kick into touch, lineout, back to Rowlands, etc., ad nauseum. The Welsh ground their way remorselessly up the touchline again, and again, and again. In this ultimate example of non-handling rugby, there were 111 lineouts – that's one every 43 seconds. The result? Oh, yes. Wales won 6–0.

Before the decade was out, the direct kick to touch outside your own 25 was a thing of the past, and insomniacs were seeking other remedies.

The Calcutta Cup of Victory Dashed

England v Scotland, Twickenham, March 1965

Hancock's try. The 85-yard dash for the line in the last minute of the game that rescued a Calcutta Cup match for England when they seemed destined – deservedly – to lose it. One of Twickenham's two most famous tries, ranking alongside Obolensky's classic against the 1936 All Blacks, and achieved by someone making his international debut. The stuff of legend and of schoolboy dreams seems out of place in a book about the chokers and jokers of the game, and so it is, looked at from England's end of the field. But if you're Scottish? Leaving aside Caledonian claims that he put his foot into touch in, conveniently, the one part of his run that fell between the lenses of the two tracking TV cameras, how could the Scots have allowed a man to escape from his 25 to run the length of the field?

Throughout the last quarter, Scottish pressure had been unremitting as they strove to add to the three points they had from a dropped goal. The game was inside injury time as Alex Hastie put into a scrum three yards out from England's line, only for England to take it against the head, and for fly-half Weston to kick clear. It was not a good kick. It went straight into the arms of Scottish winger David Whyte, who jinked in towards the posts, but lost the ball in a half-tackle, allowing Weston to recover it and fling it to Andy Hancock just inside his own 25. Hancock looked up and, realising his opposite number had come inside – or, as he said later, 'it dawned on me that Whyte wasn't opposite me' – put his head down and set off.

There were two Scots to worry about – Ian Laughland was after him from behind, and fullback Stewart Wilson was racing across to intercept. Laughland made a lunge at Hancock to tap-tackle him and succeeded in momentarily checking his stride, but Hancock was curving slightly inwards to draw Wilson towards him with the idea that he would create room for himself to swerve past on the outside. Meantime England flanker Budge Rogers was roaring up the field to make a target for Hancock and, said Hancock, 'I would certainly have given Budge the ball had he not been covered, which helped to make something of a dummy.'

Maybe it was this that caused Wilson's momentary hesitation or maybe, as Hancock charitably said, the ground was wet and he slipped slightly. For the onlookers, already stunned by the suddenness of the break-out and the dramatic reversal of fortunes, time seemed momentarily suspended as Wilson and Hancock converged at the halfway line. As Jack Bailey wrote the next day, 'It seemed that at the very least Wilson must push Hancock into touch.' But he didn't. His momentary hesitation was enough, and Hancock was round his man. 'From then on it was a dash for the line, but as I got near it, it got more and more blurred.' Hancock was also aware of pounding feet behind him. It was the indefatigable Laughland, clearly a firm believer in the most wayward of causes, who, after his failed tap-tackle, had got up and kept on coming. This was a Sassenach, after all, and every Scot knows you never let one of them out of your sight, even if you've left your claymore in the dressing room.

It was because of the pounding feet as he neared the line, Hancock said, that he flopped over without trying to get round behind the posts. In fact, Laughland had not closed enough to stop him but, after such heroics, one could hardly blame the England winger. It's worth remembering that the year of Hancock's try is poised exactly halfway between modern regimes of ultra-intensive, diet-conscious training, and the days in which Percy Royds could write, in 1928: 'Any attempt to increase the speed of rugby football is against the interest of the game in general. For most players, especially those leading an office life, the game is fast enough already.' For that matter, Willie Duggan had yet to utter his immortal dictum on the pernicious effects of training (see page 94). Perhaps it was just as well Don Rutherford's touchline conversion drifted narrowly wide. An England victory would have been a rank injustice, and poor Stewart Wilson must have been feeling bad enough already.

Forget the Rugby,
What Can We Trash Next?
The British & Irish Lions in South Africa, 1968

In the first half of the century, Lions' tours overseas had been exclusively concerned with playing rugby and spreading goodwill. True, in 1938 Blair Mayne carried out a celebrated demolition of his hotel room in Pietermaritzburg, but that was a solo performance aimed at the establishment's manager who, he felt, had insulted the squad. It was not until the 1960s, the black decade of the Lions, in which they failed to win any of their fourteen matches against South Africa and New Zealand, that the tradition of taking out frustrations on (mainly) inanimate objects was launched on its brief but heady way.

The 1960s was a period of rapidly changing social attitudes and decline in respect for authority. The players probably suffered mounting frustration as the standards of British rugby slipped further and further behind those of the southern hemisphere, compounded by what they saw, in the days before neutral officials made their appearance, as inept or biased refereeing. In the less restrained atmosphere of the times, the progression of the Lions round South Africa in 1968 had the managers of clubs and hostelries checking their insurance policies before they arrived in reception. Six years later, the manager of one South African hotel warned skipper Willie John McBride that he was going to have to summon the constabulary. Willie John considered the proposition. 'Tell me,' he said hopefully, 'will there be many police?'

This is all very well if you're a winning side, as the glorious 1974 Lions were, but their 1968 predecessors were not. The series was lost 3–0 with one match drawn, and there were times, particularly in the first Test in Pretoria, when only Tom Kiernan's kicking saved the Lions from complete humiliation. Of the 38 points they registered in the Tests, Kiernan kicked 35 – eleven penalties and the conversion of the only try scored. South Africans were not impressed by the Lions' footballing abilities and appalled by their behaviour. Some good emerged from the bottom of this pit. National squads were introduced, and coaching of skills and fitness levels at last began to be taken seriously.

When It Pays to Know Your Browns

Scotland v Wales, Murrayfield, February 1971

'Wonderful Wales win match of a lifetime!' enthused the headlines next day after John Taylor's last-kick conversion from far out gave Wales victory by 19–18. Everyone agreed that this was the game that had everything – the lead changed hands five times, and 'King' Barry John scored a try that outshone even his customary brilliance as he broke two tackles in a 25-yard run to the line. But in the enthusiasm to heap superlatives on the performance of both teams, a rather critical Scottish mistake tended to be overlooked – a mistake without which the headlines might have screamed Super Scotland rather than Wonderful Wales.

Scotland, leading 18–14, had seen wave after wave of desperate Welsh attack break down when, with full-time looming, they won a lineout just inside their own 25. Skipper Peter Brown, at number two in the line, gave the code for the throw to go to brother Gordon, the inimitable 'Broon frae Troon', at number four, only for scrum-half Duncan Patterson to countermand him with an order to hooker Billy Steele to throw to Peter. Possibly Patterson was feeling a trifle liverish on the day, and had taken exception to Gordon's famous dictum that playing in the scrum provided all the discomforts of sodomy with none of its pleasures. Whatever the reason, Peter let him know who was captain, repeated the original code for the ball to go to Gordon, spelt G-O-R-D-O-N, and prepared for the throw.

Unaware that Patterson had promptly contradicted his order for a second time, the skipper was, shall we say, mildly discomfited when Steele's throw came at him with the subtlety of a tracer bullet. He fumbled it, Scotland lost possession and at last the ball moved smoothly down the Welsh line until a long pass found Gerald Davies on the right wing. A touch on the celebrated Davies accelerator and he was in for the try, ten yards from the corner flag. Scotland 18, Wales 17 and, with the referee's whistle at his lips, everything depended on Taylor's conversion attempt. Patterson must have died a thousand deaths as he awaited the outcome. He knew what awaited him in the dressing room.

Bad Workmen Blame
Their Dogs

New Zealand v British & Irish Lions, June/July 1971

The first results of the coaching revolution that followed the disappointing performances of the Lions in the 1960s were seen on their winning tour to New Zealand in 1971, when their rising forward power gave their brilliant backs ball to play with. Before they could get into the Test series, the Lions underwent the infamous battle of Canterbury, 'probably the most publicised outbreak of on-pitch hostilities in sporting history' according to Stephen Jones, for which, the locals subsequently insisted, the Lions were responsible for repeatedly diving on the upraised boots and fists of the Canterbury players. The survivors – and there were one or two – took their revenge in the first Test with, it must be said, the willing collaboration of the All Blacks.

The Blacks came at the Lions like an avalanche in the first and last quarters, but were beaten back on every occasion. Slowly the visitors worked their way upfield, but Barry John missed two penalty opportunities to put points on the board. Then Kiwi fullback Fergie McCormick, one of the villains of Canterbury now playing in his eleventh – and last – Test, combined with his big No 8, Alan Sutherland, playing in what turned out to be his only appearance of the series, to give a boost to the Lions' aspirations. Ian McLauchlan, winning the first of his eight caps at loose-head, was destined to be on a losing Lions side only once and, in the process, to win the admiring title of 'Mighty Mouse'. Now, looking, as the *Telegraph* reported the next day, 'like the Nobby Stiles of British rugby', he caught McCormick in possession. Fergie somehow scraped the ball away to Sutherland, who, presented with this undesirable object, engaged in earnest internal debate about what should be done with it. Mighty Mouse sprang the trap of Sid Going and McCormick, who were blocking his path, barging between them to bear down on the hesitating Sutherland. Too late, the big No 8 decided to give it a hoof. Mighty Mouse charged it down, it rebounded over the line and the five-foot-eight prop fell gleefully on top of it. Props love the opportunity to score, and McLauchlan 'grinned all the way back to the halfway line'. To compound the felony, McCormick contrived to miss two All Black penalties from in front of the posts, and to complete his miserable afternoon Barry John's tactical kicking 'made him look like a pensioner – all that was missing was the wheelchair'. The Lions won 9–3 but then, in what was to be their only defeat of the tour, lost the second Test, 22–12. The series was therefore all square as the third Test kicked off in Wellington.

With their forwards dominating the lineouts in the first half, the Lions' backs had plenty of ball, and thirteen points were on the board in the first seventeen minutes. 'Jeez, they're gonna score fifty,' an anxious spectator was heard to say as John converted the second try. In fact, it was the end of their scoring and, as the second half wore on, Colin Meads, playing in the black jersey for the penultimate time, finally managed to rally his forwards. After two missed opportunities, they succeeded in working McCormick's replacement at fullback, Laurie Mains, over for an unconverted try. The score was now 13–3, and the Lions' defence was beginning to creak and look vulnerable. At this critical moment the law of the jungle was turned upside down as a boxer dog bounded joyously onto the pitch to lend the Lions a helping paw. He wasn't listed in the programme, nobody knew where he came from, but this was his first Test collar, and he was going to make the most of it.

In yet another attack, the All Blacks were moving the ball wide, and with both Mains and Alex Wyllie, Sutherland's replacement at No 8, joining the line a two-man overlap had developed. As outside centre Howard Joseph, winning his second cap, prepared to receive the ball at speed, the boxer lined up his right ankle and moved in from behind. Joseph desperately tried to step over the dog, but the damage was done. It darted away before it could be buried in a maul, Joseph fell to his knees and the pass skittered along the ground for a grateful Lion to belt down the field and lift the pressure. It was one thing to play fifteen Lions but, without a pocketful of biscuits to persuade it to change sides, quite another to play fifteen Lions *and* a dog. The All Blacks curled up in their basket and the score stayed at 13–3. By drawing the final Test 14–14, the Lions achieved a series victory over New Zealand for the first time.

Was the boxer given a special treat in its supper bowl that evening, or chained up in disgrace? No keen reporter seems to have sniffed out the truth of its ownership, but the dog had more impact in its one and only Test appearance than many another one-cap wonder. As for Howard Joseph, the third Test marked the end of his brief international career. He probably didn't choose a dog as a retirement pet.

Can I Eat Yours If You Don't Want It?

South Africa v England, Johannesburg, June 1972

England, Nul Points. England embarked on their tour to South Africa on the back of one of their worst Five Nations performances – a whitewash, in which their defence had leaked 88 points. South Africa, by contrast, were on a roll. They had gone seven matches without defeat against Australia, France and the All Blacks. Unsurprisingly, England were not expected, least of all by the Springboks, to provide stiff opposition – or indeed any sort of opposition – except in their own minds and the mind of John Pullin, their skipper. It merited mild comment, therefore, when they went through the six matches building up to the Test with an undefeated record but, as the real contest was to be played at altitude, with little preparation time, the home camp remained confident of victory. In the event, it turned out very differently.

Reporting for the *Daily Telegraph*, John Reason wrote that the Springboks 'had contributed to one of the worst performances ever put up by South Africa.' Although they won nine penalties, captain Piet Greyling destroyed confidence by rotating the kicking duties from Snyman to Sauerman to Ellis and back again, and three successful attempts by Dawie Snyman were the only points the Springboks could accumulate. England's new cap Sam Doble, meanwhile, was kicking everything that came his way and when, early in the second half, the Boks fullback, Carlson, obligingly fell over and passed the ball straight to the feet of Doble's Moseley team-mate, scrum-half Jan Webster, the resulting try gave England a ten-point lead. Doble calmly converted from the touchline to make it 18–6, and although the Springboks pulled back a penalty, they were decisively beaten. 'The alarm bells were ringing for South African rugby,' said the respected Chris

Greyvenstein, 'but a loud chorus of excuses muffled the sound and precious few heard them.'

At the farewell dinner after the match, the England players and the South African board hopped hungrily from one foot to another awaiting the appearance of the Springbok players and management. Nobody showed. Choking on the fact that they'd been well beaten by a second-rate bunch like England, they were past caring that their bad manners drew attention to their shortcomings.

An Unfortunate Incident in the Angel Hotel

Wales v New Zealand, Cardiff, December 1972

'Wales will kick themselves for all eternity about this match,' wrote John Reason after Wales lost 16–19, having exerted a second-half control that ultimately succumbed to five All Black penalties from Joe Karam and a try by prop Keith Murdoch, winning his third cap. If Wales spent the evening in self-flagellation, Murdoch celebrated his sole international try in more spectacular fashion. There was, as a New Zealand source described it, 'an unfortunate incident during the victory celebration'. To put it less discreetly, Murdoch had punched out the lights of a security guard on duty that evening at the Angel Hotel. Instead of being put under a cold shower, Murdoch found himself being frogmarched to the nearest airport and flown off for an early bath back home in Otago.

But although Murdoch left Britain as intended, he disappeared somewhere on the way home, providing journalists with a game of 'hunt the Murdoch' that keeps them happy to this day. He had disembarked en route and vanished into the Australian outback. In 1979 he saved the life of a drowning toddler on a rare visit to New Zealand, but otherwise eluded his hunters and remained hidden until Terry McLean, the Kiwi rugby writer, unearthed him living in a remote Western Australian pub. McLean's ardour for a world exclusive was metaphorically and almost literally doused when, on coming face to face with Murdoch, it was made clear to him that many things could be dumped in a nearby pool of oil, including bothersome journalists. As Murdoch was clutching a monkey wrench at the time, McLean remembered an urgent appointment elsewhere.

Then, in July 2001, as expectant hordes gathered for the decisive Wallabies–Lions third Test, Murdoch popped back into the news. A petty thief, who had broken into Murdoch's house nine months earlier, had been found dead outside the isolated township of Tennant Creek in the Northern Territory, and police were seeking Murdoch as a witness at the inquest. A newspaper got to him first and printed its conversation – or monologue – with him. Murdoch's side of the interview was at best monosyllabic. The man who had wrapped himself in a cloak of silent mystery since that bittersweet day in Cardiff back in 1972 was not about to change his spots.

'Who Wants a Goat's Head Above the Mantelpiece?'

South Africa v British & Irish Lions, third Test, Port Elizabeth, July 1974

Were Willie John McBride's 1974 Lions the greatest rugby team ever to step onto the field? You'd have a difficult time convincing South Africans they were not after the 3–0 drubbing they suffered at the claws of the Lions, which was all the more unexpected after the toothless display of their 1968 predecessors (see page 76). The 1974 Pride was without a weakness from fullback to front row. It was a team of glittering talents with men like J P R Williams, Ian McGeechan, Phil Bennett, Gareth Edwards, 'Mighty Mouse' McLauchlan, Fergus Slattery, Fran Cotton, Gordon Brown and Roger Uttley, captained and coached by two men from Ballymena, McBride and Syd Millar, who were determined to avenge the humiliations they had suffered as 1960s Lions. Unlike those teams, they were not content to rely on individual brilliance behind the scrum. They believed Tests are won by securing possession in the forwards and, with the coaching revolution that had been forced on British rugby at the end of the 1960s, they were able to ensure that no better-prepared Lions team had ever left for South Africa. 'They were mentally tougher, physically harder, superbly drilled and coached and disciplined and united,' as John Gainsford, the former Springbok centre, was to say.

The first Test was played in muddy conditions at Newlands. The game and the series were ten minutes old when Syd Millar predicted that the Lions would win the series. In that short time, he realised the Springboks had forgotten the art of scrummaging, that his forwards would be masters of the ball and that his brilliant backs would have scope for their incisive attacking play. What Millar saw the Springbok selectors also perceived and, although the Lions won by only 12–3, panic set in. Instead of trying to develop tactics to shore up the weaknesses exposed by the British visitors, they embarked on a series of inexplicable changes. In all, they were to use 33 different players,

21 of them winning their first caps, in the four-Test series.

The immediate outcome, in the second Test, was the biggest defeat in South African rugby history as the Lions ran in five tries to win 28–9 ('Lions versus lambs' in the words of one correspondent), and it was at this point that the Springbok selectors seemed, as Chris Greyvenstein said, 'to have lost control of the situation'. They dropped their best lineout specialist, John Williams, but saved their master stroke for the scrum-half position. While it was true that injuries sidelined Roy McCallum and Paul Bayvel, who had played in the first two matches, they had other specialists at their disposal, such as Barry Wolmarans and Gert Schutte, who must have sat expectantly by the phone awaiting a call to Port Elizabeth for the vital third Test. Meantime, Gerrie Sonnekus, a good No 8 forward at provincial level, was spit-roasting an ox, or whatever South African No 8s do in their spare time, when he received the news that he was in the national side for the Test – at scrum-half.

A wiser man than Sonnekus might have recalled a hamstring niggle that, to his immense distress and sorrow meant he wouldn't, alas, be fit enough to take the field. As it was, South Africa's third different half-back combination of the series had a terrible time as Sonnekus repeatedly failed to locate his fly-half and made several raking passes into space. Worse, it was the roughest match of the series, and the Lions' notorious rallying cry of 'ninety-nine' was heard on several occasions, heralding one-to-one mayhem. The Springboks competed well in the first half, nevertheless, and the half-time score was only 7–3 to the Lions, but thereafter they simply collapsed. The match was lost 26–9, the first time the Springboks had succumbed at Port Elizabeth since 1910, and the first time the Lions had beaten South Africa in a series since 1891. 'The price of a Springbok skin, once so highly valued, is of very little value at this time – who wants a goat's head above his mantelpiece?' wrote French journalist Georges Mazzocut in *L'Equipe*. Tough words that, if they were not, should have been directed to the Springbok selectors rather than the players, who scraped their way to a 13–13 draw in the final Test. As for Gerrie Sonnekus, he was only too happy to rediscover the joys of sticking your head into the scrum between the backsides of the second-row monsters, and had a belated reward for his sufferings ten years later when he won two caps against England – both at No 8 – and was on the winning side both times.

Not a Swart Move

Orange Free State v British & Irish Lions, July 1974

It was the fourteenth match of the Lions' tour and Orange Free State, like all provincial sides in South Africa (and just as in New Zealand or Australia), were laying their bodies on the line – partly, in the national interest, to try to weaken the tourists' confidence, and partly for the local pride of becoming the first side to beat the tourists. Laying your body on the line against these particular visitors was a hazardous business. The Lions were rugged, even ruthless, competitors 'who were not squeamish about resorting to obstruction, gamesmanship and even the use of boots and fists,' as a former Springbok declared. So it was hardly surprising that, by full-time, Stoffel Botha, the heavily bandaged Free State lock, looked like a man who'd just staggered away from a motorway pile-up. His suffering seemed to have been in a good cause, though, as the home side were leading 9–7, and injury time was in its third minute.

The Lions knocked on in a messy lineout, but as Botha crawled towards the resulting scrum, it was clear that he was badly concussed. Indeed, he couldn't even stand up. Under the rules prevailing, a replacement could be called up if a doctor pronounced the player unable to continue, but Free State skipper Jake Swart wasn't thinking very clearly by this stage. Maybe he too had taken such a beating from the Lions' pack that he was incapable of thought, or maybe he was supremely confident, knowing this scrum would be the last play of the game and he had only to win it and kick the ball out. He didn't call a doctor, Botha was helped off the field, and without bothering to call one of his backs into the scrum, Swart prepared to pack down.

The eight Lions drove the seven Free Staters off the ball at indecent speed before releasing the ball to J J Davies, who scooted over for a try. The referee blew for full-time and the Lions had won 11–9, leaving Swart to muse on what a silly-billy he'd been as the Lions won every one of their 22 games on tour apart from the drawn fourth Test.

Seen Through Glass Darkly

Days when the referee wished it had been somebody else out there, 1909–76

George Nepia, one of New Zealand's greatest fullbacks, was refereeing a charity match in middle age when the ball popped up invitingly before him. Unable to resist the temptation, he seized it and ran in, unopposed of course, to score under the posts. A man who relished clangers would obviously have shown himself the red card, which is what referee Gwyn Nicholls effectively did back in 1909. A Welshman and former player, Nicholls was given control, if that is the right word, of the game between England and Scotland at Richmond – the new ground at Twickenham still being six months from readiness. England lost the game 18–8, but, rather than the rugby, it was the referee's ineptitude that was the centre of post-match gossip, fuelled by Nicholls himself who said, as he left the field, 'Wasn't I awful?' Without police protection at hand, such disarming candour was probably a good tactic, but clearly he meant what he said, and never asked to referee a match again.

'Bim' Baxter might have heeded Nicholls' lesson had he had the faintest idea what was going on when he refereed the game between France and Scotland in Paris in 1913. Having actually won a game in 1911 (see page 28), the French crowds were becoming distinctly overexcited by their failure to win another when Mr Baxter supervised the 21–3 demolition of their team. They made their feelings about his decisions only too plain, or so a sensitive man would have judged. Bim, however, concluded that a French jeer or whistle, once translated, meant wholehearted approval if not, indeed, a request for an encore, and took to smiling and bowing to the crowd at every penalty. It was with some difficulty that the officials extracted him and the Scottish team from the pitch invasion that followed. The Scottish Rugby Union refused point-blank to play France again, and it was only after Kaiser Bill's squad had given them, in the Scots' opinion, a sufficiently sound roasting, that they agreed to resume fixtures. Not content with attempting to upstage World War I, Mr Baxter turned his attention to fomenting rebellion in the dominions. Managing the 1930 Lions in New Zealand, he rose unsteadily to his feet at a banquet and pronounced Dave Gallaher, captain of the great 1905 All Blacks and dead Great War hero, a cheat.

When the 1976 All Blacks visited South Africa, they were offered neutral referees for the four-Test series, but declined the offer, a decision they had good cause to regret. Most observers agree they would have won, rather than lost, 3–1 had they accepted. At the reception following the fourth Test, won 15–14 by the Springboks, the formidable Danie Craven, by then president of the SARB, was openly critical of referee Bezuidenhout's decision not to award the Blacks a penalty try following blatant obstruction by Johan Oosthuizen on his opposite centre, Bruce Robertson, after a chip through to the Springbok line. As usual, the plaintive cry of 'I didn't see it' was preferred although, strangely, Mr B had seen enough to give a penalty kick.

Also in 1976, 48-year-old Dr Andre Cuny of France was invited to referee his first international, the Wales–Scotland match in Cardiff. Alas, Dr Cuny's ageing limbs were not built to withstand ramming amidships by muscular young players, and that is precisely the fate that befell them. Despite having two international referees as his touch judges, Dr Cuny was damned if he was giving up, despite his patent inability to hobble to within hailing distance of the rucks or mauls. Like truant children, the virtually unsupervised players had a wonderful time and fists flew with gleeful freedom. Wales won 28 fights to 6, and *le pauvre* Dr Cluny was not invited back.

Experienced international referee Gareth Simmonds was in charge of the 1976 SWALEC Cup Final between Llanelli and Neath. As play entered the last quarter of an evenly balanced match, with the score tied at 18–18, Mr Simmonds awarded Llanelli a tapped penalty. Rupert Moon took it, flicked it to Emyr Lewis in front of the posts and he dropped a goal that was immediately signalled. Alas, the laws state unequivocally that the opposite must touch the ball before a score can be given. Neath queried the decision and poor Mr Simmonds realised at once what a silly boy he'd been but, having awarded the three points, all he could do was go red and look sheepish. There was no further score, and Llanelli lifted the Cup 21–18.

'Right, Lads, 80 Per Cent Commitment For 100 Minutes'

Once upon a time, training and the Irish didn't seem to go together, 1975–80

Spike Milligan loved rugby and, in particular, the rugby of his motherland. He had many stories about the game and, if he needed a new one, he had no hesitation in making it up. According to Spike, Ciaran Fitzgerald began his career as Ireland's skipper by calling the squad together for a talk. 'Let's start at the beginning,' he said, picking up a ball. 'This is a rugby ball, right?' 'Oh, Jasus,' came a voice from the back, 'you're going too fast for us.'

As we've seen (see page 14), the 1875 Irish team was credited with being 'immaculately innocent of training', and there were certainly many times in the next one hundred years when the same might have been said. Willie Duggan, Ireland's huge back-row forward who won 41 caps between 1975 and 1984, is said to have declared, brooking no opposition from those around him, that 'the quickest way to take the edge off your game is to train'. It was even claimed that he stuffed his cigarette stubs into his shorts pocket before going out to play. Perhaps such things really happened but, if so, he'd have to explain why, as a 1977 Lion in New Zealand, he benefited so well from the intensive coaching and training inevitable on such a tour that 'his barnstorming runs in the loose and control at the tail of the lineout' so impressed the All Blacks.

One feels on slightly safer ground with props of that era. Phil O'Callaghan came on as a replacement when Ireland were playing the President's XV at Lansdowne Road during the Irish Rugby Union centenary celebrations in 1975. As he went down for his first scrum, a packet of cigarettes and a lighter fell out of his pocket. He broke up the scrum, retrieved the fags and handed them to the referee with the request that he look after them until half-time because, he said, 'I'm not too keen on oranges.' These mixed emotions when it came to training may explain why Noel Murphy, the Lions coach on their 1980 South African tour, saw his charges onto the pitch with the exhortation to give it 80 per cent commitment for 100 minutes ringing in their ears.

Hwyl Go Too Far If You're Not Careful

England v Wales, Twickenham, February 1980

There were more jokers in this notorious England–Wales match than you'd find in half-a-dozen packs of playing cards, but without the smiley faces. As the Welsh side laid out its strip for the game, they were aware that they had lost only once to England at Twickenham in twenty years, not at all in Cardiff since 1963, and that they were the current champions and Triple Crown holders. Under Billy Beaumont, however, there were signs of English revival, with victories by 24–9 over Ireland and 17–13 in Paris, and the press in both countries had accordingly dragged out whatever provocations it could think of to build expectation to fever pitch by match day.

Predictably, both packs were at each other's throats from the moment the whistle blew. The first lineout turned into the kind of boxing match beloved by some fans, but deplored by the mothers of young schoolboys at rugby-playing schools and, after five minutes, referee David Burnett spoke sternly to both captains. Not sternly enough. Five minutes more, and this time the skippers were treated to the Blast Imperial, with dire warnings that the next player to offend would be leaving by the nearest exit. Of course, it's a tall order to expect the hard men up front to turn down the testosterone just like that, even after two warnings, but most rugby players remember to take their brains with them when they run down the tunnel. The last man to be sent off at Twickenham, back in 1925 (see page 44), had at least attempted to carry on his war games under cover of a good maul. Not so Paul Ringer. Just three minutes after the referee's warnings of imminent doom, he flattened England fly-half John Horton with a late, stiff-arm tackle right out in the open, and was away to the dressing room, leaving his mates to play another 67 minutes without him.

England kicked the penalty and, in theory, that should have been game, set and match to them. England did win, just, by 9–8 in what John Mason, and most of the journalists present, thought was 'a degrading war of attrition and as miserable an advertisement for the game' as there could be. Nearly everyone agreed Wales outthought England and were much the better team. The trouble was they also outfought England and, as a result, won only one-third of the total of 34 penalties awarded. This was not sensible with a kicker of Dusty Hare's reputation and ability on the other side, as he was to prove, painfully for Wales, in the dying minutes.

Wales led by four points (a try) to three at the interval, and clung to their lead for nearly half an hour of the second half, until Hare put penalty number two over to give England the lead, 6–4. Despite their best attempts to pressure and goad England into another mistake of the kind that had gifted them their first try, Wales were unable to make the breakthrough until the 77th minute when England obliged and Wales could, and should, have sealed the game.

England scrum-half Steve Smith was too slow with a clearance kick, hooker Alan Phillips charged it down, picked up, made ground and passed to Elgan Rees on the wing, who did what wingers are prone to do and took aim at the corner flag. He scooted in all right but, like Paul Ringer, had left his brain on the dressing-room peg. Instead of running in behind the posts to ensure an easy conversion to give Wales a four-point lead, and safety from any further England penalty attempts, he flopped it down in the corner and waited for the applause. Wales failed with the conversion, as they had failed with seven goal attempts, and their lead was a slender 8–6 as injury time started. In the last seconds of the game, England won a penalty as Wales went over the ball. It was way out on the touchline – the wrong side for a right-footed kicker like Hare – and the angle was narrow. With the knowledge that, if he landed the kick, England would set up an opportunity for their first Grand Slam in years, Hare kicked the goal of his life, and England indeed went on to capture the Slam by beating Scotland at Murrayfield. Lucky England. Foolish Wales.

Give Him Twenty Years and He'll Turn Out All Right

South Africa v British & Irish Lions, Port Elizabeth, June 1980

As they stood behind the line awaiting the conversion attempt that would settle the match, skipper Billy Beaumont wrapped a commiserating arm around the shoulders of the dejected Clive Woodward. 'You prat,' he said consolingly, 'you've just lost us the series.' The story's been credited to different occasions (Woodward could be brilliant, but had more than one howler to his name), but it might easily have been the third Lions Test against South Africa. The 1980 Lions were among the most popular of their breed ever to visit, owing much to Beaumont, described by his hosts as 'this most charming of men who played his heart out without ever forgetting the true spirit of the sport.' Thanks in equal measure to his opposite number, Morné du Plessis, the Test series was one of the most incident-free in modern rugby history. It was also one of the most closely fought, despite the 3–1 outcome to the Springboks.

In the 1970s, the Lions applied the hard-learned lesson that forwards win possession. They also had three-quarters of exceptionally incisive thought and movement to capitalise on the amount of ball won by their pack. In 1980, the forwards were as good as ever, if a fraction less mobile in the loose than their opponents, but the backs were not quite of their predecessors' calibre. Perhaps in consequence, there was an over-dependence on the rolling maul, and the Springboks learned to counter this predictability by spinning the ball wide to capitalise on their own outstanding runners, such as Rob Louw, Gerrie Germishuys and Gysie Pienaar.

The first Test was a thriller that seemed destined for a 22–22 draw as the stroke of time approached, only for a determined South

African drive to the line that put scrum-half Divan Serfontein over for a decisive, last-minute try. The second Test was touch and go for a long period until, during a period of intense pressure by the Lions with the score at 15–16, the ball went loose, was hacked down the field by du Plessis, and fullback Pienaar crowned an outstanding match by following up, dummying and accelerating home. The Lions never recovered from this setback, losing the try count 4–2 and going down by 26 points to 19.

Nevertheless, while the Springboks had deserved to win both matches, a tied series was still a reasonable aspiration, despite the injury toll suffered by the Lions. No fewer than eight replacements were flown out during the tour, with the result that several players were required to perform out of position. Bruce Hay went out as a fullback but, after Mike Slemen's return home, appeared on the wing; and Clive Woodward, who had formed a powerful centre pairing for England's Grand Slam side with Paul Dodge, marked his Lions career with two appearances on the opposite wing. It was the selection failure of the tour not to play Dodge and Woodward together in the centre. Even so, 'the Lions pack took the Springboks apart in virtually every facet of the game' in the third Test at Port Elizabeth, and with a half-time lead of 7–3 they looked well set to turn their fortunes around.

Alas, the second half saw a catalogue of handling and decision-making errors behind the scrum, which included Andy Irvine dropping the ball with the try line unguarded. Penalties were swapped and, with eight minutes left, the Lions were clinging to a 10–6 lead when Naas Botha kicked diagonally towards their 25. The future restorer of English rugby pride, namely one C Woodward, followed the rolling ball and helped it gently into touch, rather than belting it into Port Elizabeth High Street as an experienced wing would have done, before turning his back on it. Hitherto, the ball boys had offered the thrower a new ball for the subsequent lineout but, quick as a flash and before they had a chance to deny him use of it, Germishuys seized the ball that Woodward had nudged out and threw it in to flanker Theuns Stofberg, who ran on to draw the defence before slipping it back to Germishuys to go over in the corner and level the scores. As Woodward and Beaumont stood miserably on the line awaiting the conversion attempt, they could seek comfort from the vicious crosswind that was blowing but, in their hearts, they knew that Naas Botha – 'Nasty Booter' as the British press had christened him – missed precious little. This was no exception. His brilliant kick 'defied the wind all the way over the crossbar' and although the Lions played superbly to win the fourth Test 17–13, they had lost a series they could have drawn.

Springboks Under Siege

USA v South Africa, New York State, September 1981

The Springbok tour of New Zealand in 1981, played against a backdrop of frequently violent anti-apartheid protest, was probably the most difficult in their history. Although the quality of the rugby was superb, few matches were not disrupted, and the tourists resorted to sleeping on camp beds under the stands before a Test match to avoid the protest blockages mounted around their hotel. During the final Test, a light aircraft flew over Eden Park strafing players and spectators with flour bombs, one of which flattened Kiwi Gary Knight, briefly rendering him a horizontal All White. New Zealand won the game 25–22 and took the series 2–1.

The all-wise International Rugby Board, who must be obeyed in all things, however idiotic, then decreed that, on their way home, the Springboks should drop by the United States and play three games, the third to be an official Test Match. In a series of bizarre, protestor-dodging manoeuvres, the first two were played out, and the South Africans prepared for the culminating Test, scheduled for New York's Bleecker Stadium on the last Saturday of the visit. On the Friday, a snap decision was taken to fool the protestors (and everybody else for that matter) by playing the game that very day on a polo ground in Glenville, NY, rather than the Bleecker Stadium. The referee was not in his room at the time, so he was summarily replaced by the nearest official to hand. Non-playing Springboks were ordered to loiter conspicuously in their hotel, looking innocent, while their playing colleagues were hustled to the ground. Neither the media nor the USRFU committee were told and missed the encounter. They were not much amused.

The ground had a marked slope, so the Springboks found themselves running uphill in the second half but, as Skip Niebauer, captain of the not-so-fit US Eagles, pointed out, it was harder for the Americans because they were always doing the chasing as South

Africa won 38–7. The *S A Rugby Annual* reported attendance as 35 spectators, 20 policemen, one television crew, one reporter and no demonstrators. It was, in Chris Greyvenstein's words, 'one of the most pathetic chapters in South African sports history.'

'The Aftershave'll Flow Tonight ...'

Scotland v England, France v England, January/February 1982

If you look at a photograph of the England XV before the successful game against Australia at Twickenham with which they opened their 1982 season, you'll see flanker Nick Jeavons, sleeves demurely rolled down, standing between second row Maurice Colclough and prop Colin Smart, whose sleeves are rolled up to reveal forearms as massive as a lesser man's thighs. Colclough is looking thoughtfully at the camera, clearly contemplating future practical jokes or, just possibly, anticipating Erika Roe's famous streak, which was to enliven Twickenham's green acres an hour or so later. Smart, chin jutting pugnaciously, wears – despite being a prop – a friendly and trusting look. Within a few weeks, he was to be a sadder, wiser and decidedly sweeter-smelling man.

England's first match of the Five Nations campaign was the Calcutta Cup clash at Murrayfield and a tight, tense game was played at fast and furious pace in freezingly cold conditions, producing many unforced errors in attack. Both defences were almost faultless, blanking out any tries, and the match was settled with the boot. By half-time, England's three penalties had been answered by a dropped goal and a penalty from Scotland. The second half remained scoreless and, as injury time began, it seemed certain England would come away with the points. Scotland launched one last attack on the English line, but the ball was cleared to the halfway line where, for no discernible reason, Colin Smart saw fit to flatten Iain Paxton, who was innocent of the ball or any particular involvement in the action. A penalty to Scotland, a couple of yards inside their half, was the result, which Andy Irvine weighed up with meticulous care before finding both length and direction to secure a 9–9 draw. Poor Colin was not a popular man in Bill Beaumont's dressing room after the game, and indeed Bill felt so poorly that he retired from rugby forthwith.

At Twickenham three weeks later England crashed 15–16 to Ireland in a game more one-sided than the score suggests but, with a pack unchanged apart from the introduction of Bainbridge to partner Colclough in the second row, went on to Paris to face the fancied French. To most people's surprise they turned in a cracking performance, with the forwards allowing France only scraps of possession and restricting them to a single try. In reply England, whenever they could persuade Dusty Hare to take a break from kicking penalties, scored a first-half try from Clive Woodward and a second, in the dying minutes, from John Carleton – and the man to deliver the inch-perfect pass into his winger's hands was none other than twinkle-toed prop, Colin Smart. England thoroughly deserved their 27–15 victory and prepared to celebrate it.

Not many chronological years ago – but light years in terms of attitude now the professional era has ushered in the worship of healthy nutrition – the post-match shenanigans could easily demand of the players greater cunning and involvement than the pre-match preparations. At the banquet following their win against France, each England player had a gift of expensive aftershave from the French RFU placed on the table in front of him. Glancing furtively about him to ensure he was not observed, Maurice Colclough killed the nearest aspidistra by emptying his aftershave, and refilled the bottle with white wine, whereupon he leapt to his feet and challenged anyone to follow his example and drink his aftershave. What prop can resist a challenge, especially from a mere second-row man? Smart, thereafter to be known as Not-So-Smart, drained his present in one and, before he was halfway through the main course, was seeing flashing blue lights as the ambulance rushed him to hospital to find a niche in medical history. 'Colin may not have looked too good, but I'm told he smelled lovely,' commented Steve Smith, who'd taken over from Beaumont as England captain. 'From what I can remember,' said Colin, speaking later from his hospital bed, 'it was about par for a rugby dinner.'

He was on his feet and fit enough a fortnight later to take his place in the England side that beat Wales 17–7 at Twickenham. 'The aftershave'll flow tonight,' said Steve Smith on his way to the post-match banquet.

'Like a Pip Out of an Orange'

Australia v England, Sydney; France v Fiji, Auckland, World Cup 1987

There was never a dull moment when David Campese had a rugby ball in his hands, or at least in the approximate vicinity of his hands, and he was to star as a joker twice during rugby's inaugural World Cup. England met the Wallabies in the opening game of Pool B, a match memorable for little apart from the abject refereeing of the shapely (shapely as in spherical) Keith Lawrence from New Zealand. Midway through the second half, with the score locked at 6–6, the ball spun loose a yard or two short of the England line. Campo swept it up, took three paces to the line and dived over, arms outstretched, for what looked like a certain try. As he was in the act of coming in to land, Rob Andrew arrived and, probably fortuitously, got his left knee under the ball just before Campo landed, whence it spurted forward and over the dead-ball line. Campo lay on the ground, clutching his head despairingly in his hands, until he divined the portly arrival of Mr Lawrence, arm upraised, signalling a try. Australia won.

The quarter-final between France and Fiji was a very different game, a feast of brilliant handling, running and support play, especially from the dazzling Fijians. 'A real game of basketball,' the New Zealand TV commentator called it. Fiji were trailing 19–7 early in the second half, but threatening mayhem, when a French move broke down, the Fijian fullback pounced on the ball, whipped it out to fly-half Severo Koroduadua, and he made a clean break between two French backs into the empty French half of the pitch. Holding the ball casually in his right hand, he curved towards his left-hand touchline for the run in, the touch judge panting alongside. Although Serge Blanco was desperately striving to get across he had no hope of cutting Koroduadua off when, without warning, the ball popped out of his hand 'like a pip out of an orange' and flew into touch. Had Fiji scored then and brought the score back to 19–13, the match would have been wide open. As it was, France went through 31–16.

The Winner, on a Technical Knockout, Wayne Shelford!

New Zealand v Wales; Australia v France, World Cup semi-finals, 1987

The semi-finals of the 1987 World Cup could hardly have produced more contrasting matches – one over almost before it had begun, the other swapping the lead right up to the final, cliffhanging moments. Against Wales, New Zealand had two tries on the board before most spectators had cleared their heads from the pre-match libations. Their pack was destroying the boyos, they were winning the lineouts with ease and the Welsh defence seemed collectively still in the car park with their picnic hampers. When John Kirwan streaked in for tries number three and four it seemed a question only of whether Wales could keep the score below fifty (they did, by one point). Wales rallied briefly in the second half as John Devereux scored their only try, but it was mainly one-way traffic as the All Blacks rattled up eight tries, and the clockwork Grant Fox kicked eight goals without once disturbing his features sufficiently to indicate his pleasure. Animation finally arrived in the dying moments of the game. A hefty maul was swaying shapelessly around the Welsh half when, without warning, Gary Whetton exited left, hotly pursued by a swinging bear. The bear in question was Welsh second row Huw Richards, who landed a stinging left jab to put Whetton down for a count of five, but failed to see the cavalry, in the shape of Wayne Shelford, closing in with a haymaking right hook. As Richards adjusted himself to life in a horizontal position, he became dimly aware of a pointing arm. Fearing it might be God ordering him to another place, he was relieved to find it was merely the ref sending him off. Why Shelford didn't accompany him, only the officials could explain but, apart from the fact that there was time for Shelford to score a further try, it made no difference to the outcome.

If, leaving aside the punch-up that introduced southern hemisphere audiences to the prowess of 1980s Welsh teams in this branch of the sport, one semi-final lacked competitive tension, the one between Australia and France produced it in spades. Nobody privileged to be in Sydney that June day is likely to forget what John Reason described as 'a game that will be remembered as long as the World Cup is played'. As if to lay a foundation for the great drama of the second half, the first period was merely good. Australia had gone ahead 9–0 with two penalties and a drop goal from Michael Lynagh when, a few minutes from half-time, Lorieux ripped the ball from Troy Coker at a lineout on the Wallaby line, peeled round the front and stretched for the corner. A touchline conversion meant it was 9–6 at the interval.

A marvellous French try at the start of the second half, which saw Philippe Sella jinking diagonally through half the Australian side to touch down under the posts, gave France the lead for the first time. For the rest of the match, the score tilted first one way and then the other, until it was locked at 21–21 with under ten minutes to go. Up in the stands the Aussie coach, Alan Jones, was running his finger round the unaccustomed collar and tie he'd been required to wear for the day muttering, 'C'mon, mates, c'mon.' France's Jacques Fouroux remained impassive and unsmiling.

Then a dreadful mistake under his posts by, of all people, the great Serge Blanco, gave Lynagh a penalty to make it 24–21. Surely now it would be Australia v New Zealand in the final? Not a bit of it. Didier Camberabero kicked a penalty for a late tackle to make it 24–24. It looked as if the denouement must come in extra time until Lagisquet cross-kicked to Australia's 22, midfield, where the ball bounced in front of Campese, who seemed rather perplexed by the whole thing. Perhaps Campo was afraid of knocking on in front of the posts, or perhaps he was plotting a move of extreme cunning, but the indecision cost Australia possession. France swung play right, then left in a surging move through Champ, Lagisquet, Berbizier, Mesnel, Charvet, Berbizier and Lagisquet again, and then to Blanco who went for the corner, forgetting his injured hamstring, as if his very life depended on it. To complete the magic, Camberabero landed a perfect touchline conversion and France were through, 30–24. In the stands, a smile played briefly around Fouroux's lips. Alan Jones looked as if his collar had finally choked him but, as he said after the first shock of disappointment, it had been 'a piece of ambassadorship for the game'.

The Racing Pinks

Racing Club de Paris have the last laugh, 1987–9

It all began in January 1987. Racing Club de Paris boasted some great players in its ranks, men of the calibre of internationals Jean-Baptiste Lafond, Eric Blanc and the irrepressible Frank Mesnel. The previous year, Racing had finished second in the tough French championship race, but down in the southern heartlands of French rugby, where footballing life can be nasty, brutish and short, they were seen as a bit of a joke. How could a team from poncy Paris be taken seriously? Weren't they all a bunch of gambolling gays up there in the capital?

Right, thought the lads from Racing. You think we're a joke? We'll give you one. They went down to play Bayonne on the Spanish border, and ran onto the pitch wearing Basque berets. What might have been taken as an insult was turned to triumph by their sparkling rugby. In the semi-finals of the cup, against the mighty Toulouse, the backs turned out in long, knee-length shorts and golden boots – and won. For the final, against Toulon, they hit on what was to become their trademark, their famous pink bow ties. The Edwardian shorts may have upset Toulouse's concentration, but Toulon were of sterner mettle, and the joke misfired. Racing lost, but despite the clanger they had made their point – you can play exciting, skilful rugby with panache and good humour. They were quickly christened 'Le Show-Bizz', and for four years they had French rugby fans in thrall to their pink bow ties and their breathtaking rugby. 'Just because you play well you don't have to be serious all the time,' explained Mesnel. 'French people have always played with excitement but sometimes, before or after a match, there is too much gravity. For us, it was a release of spontaneity.'

They reached their high point at the Parc des Princes in 1989, when they met Agen in the playoff to determine the French championship. Before the kickoff, President Mitterand was formally inducted to *Le Show-Bizz*, and presented with a pink bow tie. At half-time Yvon Rousset, one of the originals but now retired, appeared, resplendent in dinner jacket, carrying out champagne and glasses on a silver salver for the refreshment of the Racing team. Racing won, and took the title. 'In the French joke, there is French seriousness,' said Mesnel.

Campo's Catastrophe

Australia v British & Irish Lions, third Test, Sydney, July 1989

'You do not play Mickey Mouse rugby in the green and gold of Australia,' roared former skipper Andrew Slack. 'Campese turns rabbit as he seeks the nearest hole,' gloated at least one member of the British media pack. But then they would gloat, wouldn't they, because David Campese had often told England in particular, and northern hemisphere teams in general, why they were pretty ordinary. What had occasioned this mixture of outrage and hilarity? Probably the most celebrated moment of indecision in rugby folklore, when Campo gifted the third Test and the series to the 1989 Lions.

The Lions had lost the first Test 30–12, but had come from behind to win the second 19–12. The deciding Test was 46 minutes old, and the Lions were trailing 12–9, when Rob Andrew attempted a drop goal which, as it dribbled off into the left-hand corner of the Wallabies in-goal area, a charitable critic might have described as misdirected. Partly because it's expected of wingers, and partly for the sheer joy of having something to do in a game being controlled by the forwards, Ieuan Evans galloped hopefully up the right touchline, while Campo, with all the time in the world, pondered his next move – or possibly where he'd have dinner that evening. His reverie was painfully interrupted by fourteen stone of flying Welshman, so he flung the ball hopefully in the direction of the nearest human being, who happened to be his fullback, Greg Martin. As it bounced off Greg's shoulder, Evans pounced gleefully for the only try of the match. It was the decisive score, and the Lions won 19–18.

'Orthodox methods have never appealed to me,' said Campo when asked why the heck he hadn't just hoofed it into touch. As Bob Dwyer said: 'He has never wanted to be restricted by the fear of failure.

His instinct is always to do things which are above the ordinary.' On this occasion things went badly wrong, but on countless others Australians and rugby-lovers everywhere had plenty of reason to celebrate Campese's skills. He is, as Stuart Barnes said of him, 'a far better man than many people give him credit for.'

'So Foul and Fair a Day
I Have Not Seen'

Scotland v England, Murrayfield, March 1990

March 1990, and the entire array of northern hemisphere prizes was up for grabs as England marched north to Murrayfield – Calcutta Cup, Triple Crown, Championship and Grand Slam. But points mean prizes, and without them you win nothing – a simple equation England had forgotten and Scotland had not. The Scots had beaten France convincingly enough, 21–0, but had squeaked home by three points in Dublin and only four, in front of their home crowd, against Wales, giving them a total of 47 points to date. England, meantime, had won all the plaudits, exerting domination up front as a prelude to releasing their silken backs and running in eleven tries, putting 83 points on the board in the process. No contest, as far as most observers were concerned, and England made – or appeared to make – the fatal mistake of believing them. If there's one thing the Scots really relish, it's being taken for the underdog.

The scene was set even before the referee had blown for the kickoff. England trotted onto the pitch to the anticipated farrago of jeers and whistles. They were kept waiting, savouring their reception, until Scotland adjudged them nicely tenderised, and then David Sole emerged at the head of his clansmen marching, memorably, with measured step and jutting jaws to a drawn-out crescendo of cheering. We can never be sure how much this rattled England, and whether or not it was responsible for their subsequent misadventures, but what was wholly predictable was that Scotland's back-row trio would play to the limits of legality in harassing anything that moved within yards of England's scrum. This was a familiar tactic that England would have been expecting, and they were probably not all that surprised to find themselves trailing behind two Craig Chalmers' penalties before Jerry Guscott made a gloriously clean break to score the first try of the match.

With the England forwards now beginning to drive back their

opposite numbers and lay siege to the Scottish line, England fans settled back to await the avalanche of tries that must follow. England nearly scored a pushover try, but somehow the scrum seemed to keep collapsing. How odd. As Oscar Wilde might have said, 'One collapsed scrum might be regarded as unfortunate, but three really did merit the firing squad.' England kept being given penalties but didn't seem to know what to do with them. Kick at goal? Tap kick? Give it to the backs? Where was the captain to take the decisions? Indeed, who was the captain? Will Carling, it said in the programme, but it looked from afar as if Brian Moore was in charge. Perhaps England were expecting to be awarded a penalty try and were looking for seven, rather than three, points. If that was the thinking it was misguided. Fullback Simon Hodgkinson had already kicked 39 of England's 83 points in their three previous Tests. Not once was he given the ball in the first half as England repeatedly spurned easy penalties and the points that went with them.

Meantime, at the other end, Scotland accepted their chance of a third penalty, so England turned round 4–9 down. Even now, Scottish fans were hardly daring to hope that the tartan fires could be kept fully stoked for another forty minutes. Surely, thought the English ones, normality will be restored in the second half?

The fires were not merely stoked, they erupted like Krakatoa within minutes of the restart, and England were the ones to shovel on the fuel. Scotland's kickoff went out on the full. England took the scrum at halfway but Moore's fast strike cannoned off Mike Teague back into the scrum, giving the Scots the put-in. Back came the ball, via John Jeffery and Gary Armstrong, to Gavin Hastings, who chipped delicately to the right wing for Tony Stanger to leap high, secure the ball and dive over. A nine-point advantage, especially with England the opponents, was one any Scot would back himself to defend. Helped by an increasing catalogue of errors as England grew desperate in the face of unyielding defence, Scotland emerged thoroughly worthy winners, 13–7, and scooped the entire trophy cabinet to set off one of the most prolonged rugby parties in their history. To own a bar in Rose Street that night was a short cut to contented retirement.

Although we didn't know it at the time, England were to become experts at tossing away the Grand Slam as the decade came to a close (see page 122).

Who's Right? You, Me or the Ref?

New Zealand v Scotland, second Test, Auckland, June 1990

Things were shaping up nicely for Scotland after 85 fruitless years of trying to register their first victory over the All Blacks. Although the northern hemisphere Grand Slam holders had gone down 31–16 in the first Test of their 1990 tour of New Zealand, they were well worth their 18–15 lead in the second Test over opponents unbeaten in their last twenty matches. As the game entered its last quarter they had, despite the filthy conditions, scored two tries, from Tony Stanger and Alex Moore, against one by the All Blacks, and Gavin Hastings' kicking was as sure as Grant Fox's.

Scotland were awarded a penalty in their own 22. 'I remember thinking how wet and slippery the ball had become as I kicked it,' said Hastings and indeed, though he got length on his kick, accuracy eluded him and the ball was caught by Kiwi fullback Kieran Crowley, who simply punted it back in Gavin's general direction. Hastings went to gather the bouncing ball and turned to find All Black flanker Mike 'Bruiser' Brewer virtually on top of him. 'How he wasn't penalised for being at least sixty metres in front of Crowley I'll never know,' commented the rueful Hastings when it was all over. As he tried to sidestep the onrushing Brewer, Gavin slipped on the wet turf and was buried, first by Bruiser and, in short order, by most of the rest of the Blacks. Scottish support was conspicuous by its absence. Referee Derek Bevan penalised Scotland for not releasing – fat chance – and there was never much likelihood of Grant Fox missing that, or a later penalty as New Zealand squeezed past Scotland 21–18.

Was Bruiser offside by sixty-odd metres? 'The rule was changed,' he explained, 'so that you could actually be in front of the kicker, as long as you were at a distance of ten metres from the ball when it was retrieved. As soon as the defender moved five metres you could tackle him, as long as you began ten metres away. It was definitely within the rules.' So who was right? Wuz Scotland robbed, or had they simply not done their homework on yet another lorry-load of rule changes?

The Anglo-Saxon Conspiracy
Theory Gets an Airing

France v England, Paris, February 1992

There's nothing the French like better than taking refuge in the grand Anglo-Saxon conspiracy theory – that on the rugby pitch, and possibly in life generally, the British expend all their energies in devising plans to thwart French grandeur. The fact that Scots, Welsh and Irish are Celts, not Anglo-Saxons, disturbs this sense of grievance not a jot. England arrived at the Parc des Princes in 1992 having beaten Scotland and Ireland, and beginning to anticipate a second successive Grand Slam. Brian Moore had warmed the temperature by telling the French press beforehand that their rugby was dirty because their club rugby was dirty – a view held by many, but not calculated to have the French chuckling in avuncular pleasure when the whistle went. Worse still, the English support in the stands was massive. How they had got their tickets, no-one could say, but throughout the game the volume of support for England was consistently higher than that for the home team. The poor man charged with refereeing the ensuing carnage was Stephen Hilditch who, coming from Ireland, was not noted as a prolific architect of Anglo-Saxon conspiracies, but who was to be denounced as a villain throughout France.

The scrum was a roughhouse from the word go and, as usual in those dark recesses, the outside world remained ignorant of who was doing what to whom. From those parts of the game that could be seen clearly by the masses watching in the stands and on television it was, as John Mason reported, 'a mighty performance by England in a match which, for an hour at least, had a score of sublime moments.' On the face of it, the trouble began when, with France leading 4–3, the referee awarded a penalty try to England. Twice, England had heaved for a pushover try, and twice the scrum had collapsed. On the first occasion, the ball had squirted out to Dewi Morris, who had caught it in an offside position, only for the scrum to be reset.

It seemed to some observers that the second collapsed scrum was more accidental than deliberate, and it goes without saying that that's how the French would have seen it. France never regained the lead although, it must be said, their selectors were probably the real villains of the piece for choosing a thoroughly unbalanced pack with, Laurent Cabannes apart, no presence in the lineout. The more they felt themselves being outplayed, the more frustrated they became.

Sixteen minutes into the second half, with England leading 18–7, Rob Andrew and French skipper Philippe Sella left the field after an accidental clash of heads and, with the removal of Sella's calming influence, the match descended first into farce and then into mayhem. Attempting a scissors move in their own half, fly-half Alain Penaud and substitute Jean-Luc Sadourny contrived to run into each other at full tilt. While the spectators were wiping away the tears of hilarity, Will Carling seized the loose ball and, four pairs of hands later, Rory Underwood sped over for England's third try to make the score 24–7 and put the game beyond French reach.

'Gallic marbles take French leave' was the heading in the *Telegraph's* report the following Monday, describing what it called 'the slide towards madness and mayhem' in the last ten minutes. 'French ranks were almost in anarchy,' reckoned Stephen Jones as, first, loose-head Grégoire Lascubé, a police inspector during the week, was dismissed when touch judge Owen Doyle spotted him doing a fandango on Martin Bayfield's head. 'That sent the French wild,' said Brian Moore, 'and they lost all reason and sanity.' Hooker Vincent Moscato, moving to take over Lascubé's propping duties, came into the scrum with tears of rage pouring down his face, and screaming with anger. It was said that referee Hilditch could see what was about to happen, and warned him several times in French not to head butt, but he was beyond control and, within a few minutes of Lascubé's departure, Gimbert was left as the sole representative of the French front row. England scored again to make the final score 31–13 and, not for the first time in Paris, a police escort was needed to get the referee safely off the field. Lascubé and Moscato were both banned for six months, and Bernard Lapasset, President of the French Rugby Federation, publicly ordered the French team to put its house in order. That the French team of the early 2000s had both flair and discipline may owe much to the mayhem in Paris ten years previously.

Weasels With
Attitude – and Appetite

**Skulduggery mainly, but not exclusively, in the front row,
1966 & 1990s**

'Props are as crafty as a bag of weasels,' as Bill McLaren famously
said. What goes on in that front row remains a mystery to those not
in the union. Ciaran Fitzgerald recalls winning the ball twice against
the head in one of his first matches as a hooker. 'The next thing I
knew I was being carried off.' But from time to time what goes on in
the set pieces spills over into the relatively open ground of ruck and
maul, which is as near as a prop can get to stripping naked in public.

In July 1994, during the second Test between the All Blacks and
South Africa in Wellington, Springbok prop Johan Le Roux had clearly
been driven to distraction whenever the front rows went down by
the mouthwatering proximity of Sean Fitzpatrick's left ear. Unable
to contain himself after Fitzpatrick had driven him off the ball in a
ruck, Le Roux helped himself to a large bite, whereupon Fitzpatrick
complained bitterly to referee Brian Stirling, presumably on the
grounds that the order had not been placed in advance and wasn't
ready to be served. With a dreamy look on his face and smacking
his chops contentedly, Le Roux was asked to leave the restaurant
and finish his meal in private. True to the code of *omertà* observed
by all stout members of the front-row mafia, Fitzpatrick was saying
nothing after the match. Despite the blood still dripping from the
wound, and the fact that the incident had already been replayed
to the world at large a hundred and one times on TV, Fitzpatrick's
grizzled face wore no more than a look of puzzled incomprehension
as the press clamoured for details. Le Roux was quite rightly – and
promptly – sent home in disgrace by the South African management.

Not that this was the first time ear tartare had appeared on the
menu. During Australia's tour of Britain in 1966–7, Wallaby hooker
Ross Cullen developed a sudden passion for a chunk of a hunk called

Ossie Waldron playing, at the time, in the Oxford University pack. Cullen was likewise returned to Australia earlier than anticipated and, deprived of a steady diet of tender northern hemisphere flesh, was never again seen on a rugby pitch.

Clearly, then, there are limits to the violence that even props can be allowed to practise. Or are there? In New Zealand they seemed to have a slightly different attitude in the 1990s, roughly along the lines: Belt the hell out of a fellow Kiwi – bad; knock seven bells out of anyone else in the world – you're a hero. All Black prop Richard Loe had already been in trouble in the first Test of 1992 against Australia, when Sam Scott-Young had required fifteen stitches after an unscheduled meeting in a not-very-dark alleyway. The New Zealand tour management ignored a call for his suspension. A fortnight later, Loe was at it again. As Wallaby winger Paul Carozza lay defenceless on the ground after scoring the first of his two tries, Loe smashed his elbow into his face and broke his nose. 'If Loe gets out of this one he's a miracle man,' said Aussie coach Bob Dwyer. 'It was late, and it was cowardly – a disgrace to the game.' It was all of those things, and although neither referee nor touch judge admitted to seeing it, the ubiquitous TV cameras duly had it on tape. The response of the New Zealand management was again dead silence. How Loe can you get? At least Australia won the game 19–17, and the series 2–1, so one kind of justice was done. And Loe got a degree of comeuppance later, when he was suspended for gouging a fellow New Zealander in a domestic game. Now that is naughty.

The double standards of the All Black tour management were exposed again at Twickenham the following year, although this time the guilty party was Jamie Joseph, a flanker. New cap Kyran Bracken was having a storming game at scrum-half for England when, still in the first half, Joseph felt in need of a little dancing practice. With Bracken obligingly helpless on the floor, and play at a safe distance, Joseph singled out the scrum-half's ankle for a *pas de deux* or three. Speaking from his crutches the next day Bracken, with masterly understatement, said, 'Having seen the video, I realise that what happened could have been avoided.' Having seen the video, the New Zealand tour management followed their hallowed tradition and did precisely nothing. This time, though, they paid the price. On return, manager Neil Gray was sacked.

On a Wing and a Prayer

Wales v England, Cardiff, February 1993

In these days of non-stop, fifteen-man rugby you're as likely to find a wing three-quarter in the thick of a maul as on the wing, and the very least that's expected of him is to impersonate a Sherman tank in defence. In quaint, pre-professional days, though, a wing could spend large parts of the match gazing enviously at the ball inextricably locked in the capacious paws of the forwards and wondering if, by chance, the ball might come his way. Even before World War I, this had been the fate of such flying wingers as Cyril Lowe, which moved P G Wodehouse to write a poem on the question, concluding: 'And incredulous reporters shouted out to the three-quarters: "Did we dream, or did you really pass to Lowe?"' Rory Underwood, England's flying winger of the 1980s and 1990s, like Lowe a fighter pilot, must often have found it hard to keep his concentration at the highest pitch as his pack rumbled up and down the field. This is the best excuse one can find for a couple of hoof-in-mouth moments perpetrated by Rory, both against Wales at the Arms Park, and both of which cost England the match.

In 1989, England had somehow contrived to be 9–6 ahead at half-time. Their performance on a sodden pitch had been moderately clueless, although, in fairness, inept refereeing (or lack of it) had reduced their main attacking weapon, the lineout, to a shambles. From the restart, Wales returned England's kickoff with a diagonal kick to the open side, and Underwood dropped it. Wales heeled from the resulting scrum and sent an overlong up-and-under to Rory, who caught the ball on the 25. Observers are unanimous that he did not actually pull out a scrap of paper and jot down his options, but when he finally elected to throw a long pass to fullback Jon Webb, he failed to notice his scrum-half, Dewi Morris, blocking the route of the ball. Wales happily hacked the resulting loose ball over the line, where Mike Hall flopped on it, and Wales, gifted a 12–9 lead, applied their tactical nous to keeping England penned in their own half, and well away from any retaliatory scoring chances.

By the time of the 1993 game, Ieuan Evans, playing opposite Rory Underwood, was celebrated as the man who played the lead in Campo's Catastrophe (see page 112). Here was someone who, if he saw a loose ball in the next parish, would hunt it down relentlessly, just in case. As half-time approached, England were ahead 9–3. Two years earlier, they had at last laid their 28-year hoodoo at the Arms Park to rest, and in their last three encounters with Wales had scored 83 points while conceding only 12 in reply. Now, they were looking for a third successive Grand Slam, and their mighty forward machine appeared to have this game well in hand. Cometh the hour, cometh the clanger.

England were threatening the Welsh line once again when flanker Emyr Lewis booted the ball downfield in a bid to gain a moment's breathing space. Underwood turned and trotted back to gather the loose ball, glancing inside him to satisfy himself there were no chasers. Unfortunately for him, he forgot to look *outside* and was the only person, among all those in the stands or watching on television, who remained blissfully unaware of the perfect storm gathering just behind him. In a Christmas pantomime, there would have been a collective shout of 'Behind you, Rory!' but this was Christmas in February for the Welsh, and any advice they had to offer was not in a language in which he was fluent. With a barely perceptible shrug of the shoulders implying he'd done it all before, Ieuan flicked off the safety catch and rocketed up on Rory's blind side, gathered in the ball, and was away to the line before you could say J J Williams. As Brian Moore recalled: 'Rory had hours, it seemed, to react, but he moved with mystifying slowness.'

There was nothing mystifying about the scoreline, which now read Wales 10, England 9, and that was the way it stayed throughout a nerve-jangling second half. Having had their stocking so unexpectedly filled by Santa Rory, the Welsh weren't letting go of the tangerine in the toe and ensured Cardiff one of its happiest nights of celebration in years. As John Mason wrote the next day, 'Losing in Cardiff again felt just like old times!'

I'm Sure Someone Gave Me a Book of Rules Once ...

New Zealand v British & Iron Lions, first Test, Christchurch, June 1993

The spirits of the 1993 Lions sank a little when they learned who was to referee their first Test against the All Blacks. Australia's Brian Kinsey won few marks from the players when in charge of both Tests in England's drawn 1990 series in Argentina. 'We had never rated him one bit in the England camp,' said Brian Moore. Within ninety seconds of the kickoff at Lancaster Park the forebodings were to prove more than justified. Grant Fox put up a beautiful cross-kick for Frank Bunce to catch and fall on over the Lions' line but Ieuan Evans, alive to the situation, had gone up with Bunce and was embracing both him and at least a third-share of the ball like a dog clinging to the postman's ankle. The entwined pair crashed to the ground over the line and awaited arbitration. Mr Kinsey, who was 'not one of the quickest referees around' according to a fellow Australian, was some way behind the play but, on panting up, gave a try. He had, he said later, been given an unofficial indication by the touch judge. Photos and TV replays, depending on their angle, showed differing claims to ownership of the ball as it was grounded, and the law is perfectly clear that 'Where there is doubt as to which team grounded the ball in-goal, a scrummage shall be formed five metres from the goal line.'

Despite this early setback, and their own poor performance during the first fifteen minutes, the Lions gradually took control of the match and were 18–17 ahead in the last minute of normal time, when up popped Mr Kinsey again. Dean Richards had enveloped Frank Bunce, turned him in classical fashion and the ball was released. Almost immediately bodies dived over both Bunce and Richards, trapping them both – one All Black, indeed, dived several feet in front of the ball in attempting to retrieve it. Unperturbed, Mr Kinsey, after a few moments mentally reviewing what he remembered of the law, gave a penalty against the Lions for holding the ball. As skipper Gavin Hastings said: 'Why would he be holding the ball in that position at that time?' Good question, but it finished 20–18 to the Blacks all the same.

A Night of Shame

Canada v South Africa, World Cup Pool A, Port Elizabeth, June 1995

The opening match of the 1995 World Cup between Australia and hosts South Africa at Newlands showed rugby at its best. It was preceded by a stylish and good-natured inaugural ceremony designed to advertise the rainbow diversity of a country newborn after the oppression and rancour of apartheid, and it reduced many onlookers of all nationalities, but especially those supporting the green and gold, to tears of pride. The rugby that followed ensured that South African emotions remained buoyant. Australia were expected to win and when, after penalties had been exchanged, Michael Lynagh scored for the Wallabies, it looked as though expectations would be fulfilled. Pieter Hendriks' try shortly before half-time, though, gave the Springboks a 14–13 interval lead and a ray of hope that their second-half pressure converted into victory. Joel Stransky scored in all the four possible ways – a try, a dropped goal, a conversion and four penalties – as South Africa won 27–18. After the game, skipper François Pienaar presented his jersey to Nelson Mandela who, with nice political judgement, called the South African team 'my Springboks'.

The side was now on such a high that everyone expected them to coast through their remaining pool matches against Romania and Canada. The Springboks began their game against Romania brightly enough and were soon 8–0 ahead, at which point Johan Roux delivered a perfect cross-kick for unmarked Chris Roussow to take and score, only to see it go straight through his hands into touch. From that point the game staggered from bad to worse and, although South Africa won 21–8, the Romanian skipper, Tiberiu Brinza, was moved to announce to a slightly perplexed press corps that 'it certainly was a moral victory for our team.'

Four days later, the circus moved on to Port Elizabeth for the final Pool A match against Canada. 'This,' Chris Greyvenstein was to write, 'was South Africa's night of shame. After the team's exhilarating ascent to glory on the opening day of the World Cup it should all have been so different.' A night of shame it certainly was, but one for which the Canadians bore at least as much blame as the Springboks. Things had got off to a bad start even before this evening match got under way. The night before there had been three successive power failures, a warning that was apparently ignored, and a further blackout delayed the kickoff by three-quarters of an hour, drawing out the tension for players and officials and ensuring an ill-humoured crowd.

This was the first time Canada and South Africa had met in an international and both teams were now playing for a quarter-final place. From the first minute, the Springbok scrum had the beating of their opponents, and dominated the set pieces and the lineouts. Content to deny Canada possession, they were 17–0 ahead by the interval thanks to two converted push-over tries from Adriaan Richter and a Stransky penalty. Soon after the restart, Stransky stretched the lead with another penalty, and there the numerical scoring finished. From then on it was a question of who won the punch count.

Showing plenty of pride, the combative Canadians forced their way back into the game, 'hurling wave upon wave of attack against the Springbok line'. In keeping with South African tradition, their defence was magnificent, but the physical aggression, which had been present from the start, was building to enormous proportions. Six minutes from the end, it exploded. As the ball when into touch, Winston Stanley of Canada and Springbok Hendriks collided in a petulant shoving match that had them rolling up against the advertising boards, each trying to find an opening to practise his right hook. There the matter might, and should, have ended, but it was all too much for Canada's fullback Scott Stewart, who came steaming in from afar and at pace to launch himself at Hendriks, apparently determined to show him how an uppercut should be delivered. In a flash, players from both sides plunged into the fray not, it seemed, to restrain their hotter-headed colleagues, but as contestants for the heavyweight championship of the world. The violence was uncontrolled.

When referee David McHugh, the touch judges and the various officials scattered around the place finally managed to restore a semblance of calm, the retributions began. Springbok hooker James Dalton, Canada's captain and fly-half Gareth Rees and their prop Rod Snow were all sent off – an unhappy record for a Test match. Hannes Strydom also had to leave the field with a damaged eye, and the formalities of the remainder of the game were played out with uncontested scrums until the referee's whistle brought the proceedings to a welcome end. The three dismissed players were subsequently suspended for thirty days by the World Cup Disciplinary Committee, ensuring that Dalton would miss the rest of the competition, and when the Springboks appealed against the decision, the committee promptly cited two other players – Hendriks and Stewart – each of whom also received suspensions. It was, by far, the blackest point of South Africa's year, but within three weeks it had turned to sunshine as they went on to win the World Cup.

Would That Be Jonah as in Whale?

England v New Zealand, World Cup semi-final, Newlands, June 1995

England travelled to the 1995 World Cup with a reputation as relentless scrummagers who would squeeze the life out of the opposition and whose immobile rugby, if they won, would be a disaster for the future of the game. In the pool matches they seemed tense and tired, and plumbed the depths of static performance as they ground out a 24–18 win over Argentina in what Stuart Barnes called 'the longest eighty minutes of rugby I can remember'. Having qualified, they relaxed a little and when, in the quarter-final against Australia, they avenged their 1991 Final defeat, thanks to Rob Andrew's stunning dropped goal two minutes into injury time, they suddenly found the whole world, and particularly the South African press, grateful to them for clearing the cup-holders out of the way. Now they were talked about as likely finalists as they contemplated the All Blacks in the semi-final. Not many people stopped to ask themselves the obvious questions. Why had the Australians still been in the lead four minutes from full-time if the English pack was so dominant? Why had England scored only one try, and that the result of a Wallaby error and, above all, why had Jeremy Guscott and Rory and Tony Underwood been left as little more than defensive numbers throughout the game?

As England headed for Cape Town and their semi-final against New Zealand, the tiredness and tension of the early stages of the tournament were replaced by smiles and confidence. The All Blacks were, of all things, being treated as the underdogs, and England seemed happy to go along with the idea! They made no special plans for the surprise package New Zealand had brought to the World Cup, a twenty-year-old giant of nineteen stone, who could run like the wind and had a pretty nifty sidestep, called Jonah Lomu. To quote Stuart Barnes again: 'An England side intent on static rugby was bad enough, but one that underestimated a side of New Zealand's calibre was a recipe for disaster.' Had you asked the former All Black coach, John Hart, he would have agreed. 'I saw England prepare before the game and it was obvious that they had overrated their ability to beat the All Blacks. They believed in themselves too much.' Or, as Mike Gibson said (see the Foreword), their self-confidence was misplaced, and that is the stuff of which clangers are made.

New Zealand kicked off, and made elaborate preparations to kick the ball right before suddenly switching the kick to the left for Graeme Bachop to gather and pass to Lomu. A day or two earlier, Jonah's opposite number, Tony Underwood, had been seeking help from the team psychologist in answering the media's insistent questions about how he planned to stop Lomu. He might have used the time better had he called for practice sessions to work out the answer for himself. Tony, half Lomu's size, was confronted by what must have seemed like a bull elephant on the rampage, and was swept under its hooves. Will Carling barely laid a finger on Jonah, and Mike Catt was simply overrun as the first try was scored in less than ninety seconds. A few seconds more, and a sweeping passing movement out of the Kiwis' own 22 ended with Josh Kronfeld going over for a second try, and the score was 12–0 after three minutes.

It could only get worse, and it did. Lomu added a third try, his second of what would be four, and Rory Underwood had yet to touch the ball. When Jonah completed his hat-trick, the scoreboard read 35–3 and the England juggernaut had been 'reduced to a shambling disaster'. At this moment, when both hope and pressure had vanished like smoke on the wind, England finally began to play rugby, real rugby, of the kind with which we have since grown happily familiar. Of course, the All Black foot was off the pedal by now, but at last ambition and vision were embraced. Rory scored with the first pass he received, Will Carling ran in two, and then Rory grabbed a fourth on the stroke of time. The final scoreline was 45–29, and although nothing could disguise the thrashing the Kiwis had handed out, one can see with the benefit of hindsight that this was the moment when a new and different vision for the future of English rugby was born.

Back Tosses His Toys Out of the Pram

Bath v Leicester, Pilkington Cup Final, Twickenham, May 1996

'Leicester and Bath bicker like fishwives,' commented journalist Andrew Longmore at the end of the 1995–6 seasons, which saw Bath do the Cup and League double for the fourth time, as they pipped Leicester by a point for the Championship, and took the Cup – for the tenth time – at the very last gasp. And what a last gasp it was – 'an ending worthy of the Keystone Cops'.

For ninety minutes the Final had been, in Mick Cleary's words, 'a game that stumbled and meandered, struggling for shape and definition.' Leicester scored the only try of the first half, and their judicious blend of attacking rugby from solid defence made them look the likely winners until, in the second half, they went into their defensive mode, ignoring their backs. They added a second try to take the lead 15–9, but the game became static and even a little boring. 'As has been our wont this season,' their coach, Ian Smith, was to admit after it was all over, 'when opportunities have occurred we haven't made the best of them.' The caution that came over them in the second half was to cost them dear in the last minute of the game.

Bath attacked repeatedly, and four times consecutively Leicester went over the top, cynically killing the ball. It was too much for referee Steve Lander, king of the penalty try. A warning had been issued before the 1995–6 season that persistent killing of the ball in defence of one's line would reap the ultimate deterrent. Lander had reminded both teams before the game and, as the Leicester spate of serial killing continued, warned skipper Dean Richards again. If Leicester expected to be forgiven like the prodigal son, they were sadly mistaken. He awarded a penalty try that Jon Callard converted, and it was to Bath the fatted calf was given, 16–15. It was all too much for Neil Back, who shoved Lander to the ground from behind. When it came to the disciplinary hearing, Back didn't have a leg to stand on. Unfortunately for him, Steve Lander hadn't either. Back was duly and inevitably suspended for six months by the RFU (who might have preferred to suspend him by his thumbs), so the net result was that Leicester lost both Cup and League by a point, and Back to a compulsory count.

'Bokke, O Bokke!'

South Africa v British & Irish Lions, Cape Town, June 1997

The image of a beaming François Pienaar holding aloft the 1995 World Cup in the presence of Nelson Mandela, famously wearing the Springbok shirt as a signal to the world that multiracial rugby was now king in South Africa, was deceptive. Accusations of racism were now being levelled at the sport, a secret tape recording had embroiled former coach Andre Markgraaff in the notorious 'kaffir' row, and the government was insisting on a full investigation of such matters. Not long before the summer of 1997, the talented and diplomatic Pienaar had been stripped of the captaincy in favour of Gary Teichmann, and now the Lions, on their first visit to South Africa for seventeen years, were awaited. Afrikanerdom saw the coming Test series as a rearguard action to re-establish the old values of Springbok rugby, and recover what it saw as its purity. For those whose interest was confined simply to rugby as a game, the series might well hinge on the scrum-half duel between Rob Howley and Joost van der Westhuizen. Former Aussie coach Alex Evans reckoned Howley was 'capable of coming back from South Africa one of the best scrum halves in the world, if not the best', and Mick Cleary forecast he would be Man of the Tour, so when his collarbone was dislocated on the eve of the first Test, it seemed the Lions had been dealt a devastating blow. They refused to betray a smidgen of concern. Wasn't Matt Dawson a key player alongside Gregor Townsend in Ian McGeechan's strategy at Northampton? Why should it change things now that the pair were in red shirts?

If Matt Dawson was an inevitable selection, propping Keith Wood with Tom Smith and Paul Wallace was a brave one. Within fifteen seconds, they found themselves packing down against Os du Randt and Adrian Garvey. The Lions' pack was shoved back not once, but twice. 'Welcome to the southern hemisphere,' mocked the crowd, as they anticipated an afternoon of Springbok forward domination. 'The hit came so quick,' said Keith Wood, 'and I thought, "Shit, this is going to be harder than we thought." We hadn't concentrated as hard as them, or matched their intensity. From then on we did.' As the Lions conceded a second scrum close to their own line, the crowd yelled, 'Pushover!' But this time, the Lions held, and they went on holding the scrum until in the second half it was, in the eyes of one observer, 'working like a vice'.

The Lions turned round one try down, but 9–8 ahead thanks to Neil Jenkins' crushing accuracy whenever a penalty was within range. Then the Springboks nudged ahead 13–12 with a second try, created by the outstanding Teichmann, and stretched again to 16–12 as Henry Honiball landed a penalty. Jenkins dragged the Lions back to within a point. There were eight minutes left.

Supported by Lawrence Dallaglio, the shiny-domed Wood drove forwards from a lineout, 'like a potato on speed', and won a scrum. As the ball was held in the back row by Tim Rodber, Dawson invited the opposition to come offside, but the Springbok flankers stayed down. A second's pause for thought and then, scooping up the ball, Dawson set off diagonally right, pulling Teichmann and Kruger with him. That's when the South African skipper, in a split second, lost the plot, the match and, as it turned out, the series. Consciously or not, Dawson mimicked the very action with which Teichmann had set up the second Springbok try. Lifting the ball in his right hand, he made as if to pass over his shoulder. Both Teichmann and Kruger hesitated, looking to intercept the pass they anticipated. Instead, Dawson sold them the biggest dummy you'll ever see on a rugby pitch and was away to the line, outrunning fullback Andre Joubert to touch down as Van der Westhuizen and Andre Venter piled on top of him. Teichmann stood there, head bowed, hands on hips, knowing that in the unforgiving eyes of Afrikanerdom, he'd been made to look a novice. Sure enough, the headlines next day in the white press suggested the sky had fallen. 'Bokke, O Bokke!' lamented one. 'Hungry Lions beat tame Boks in tough Test,' read another. 'Boks: What went wrong?' asked a third, concluding that arrogance, complacency, poor selection and regional rivalries were all to blame.

The Lions won again in Durban a week later to settle the series ahead of the third encounter. Afterwards, in the scrummage of the press room, a fine man and outstanding rugby player asked for a coke at the bar but was ignored for several minutes. It was Gary Teichmann.

The Tussle in Le Toulzac

Brive v Pontypridd, Pool C, Heineken European Cup, September 1997

'We have marvellous support and are known as a family club,' said Cenydd Thomas, chief executive of 1997 Welsh champions, Pontypridd, when interviewed by *Rugby News*. 'Whenever we play away the club treasurers are rubbing their hands together and that speaks volumes.' Unfortunately, he didn't explain for what purpose they were rubbing their hands together. Pontypridd had been drawn in Pool C of the European Cup dubbed, in the clichés so beloved of the average hack, the Pool of Death. Nevertheless, Ponty were reckoned to be in with a shout because, as *Rugby World* noted with uncanny foresight, their new signings enabled them to pack a greater punch behind the scrum. *Rugby World* omitted to predict the uses to which this greater punch would be put.

Very few front-line rugby correspondents made the journey to Brive for the away leg of Pontypridd's tie. There were plenty of other big games being played and, along with many other ties, it rated only a couple of centimetres at the foot of the sports pages next day. 'Even a double sending-off could not overshadow a rousing climax as Patrick Lubungu scored a try in the dying seconds to snatch back the lead Ponty had taken late in the second half when Kevin Morgan charged down Christophe Lamaison's kick and followed up to score,' was a typically brief account. The sendings-off had happened in the 27th minute, when Dale Mcintosh, Ponty's Kiwi No 8, and flanker Lionel Mailler of Brive were given their marching orders for fighting. They were not, by any means, the only combatants. Indeed, 27 of the 30 players were involved in a mass brawl, and the mischievous Mcintosh milked the menacing atmosphere by making mocking gestures at the Brive crowd as he departed to put his feet up. 'There were,' observed Donald McRae, 'occasional outbreaks of rugby' on the pitch, but the all-embracing brawl on the field was that evening to spread like a GM crop into Le Toulzac, a local bar where the Brive players often enjoyed a post-match drink.

The events in the bar that Sunday night ensured that a couple of centimetres on the back pages became many column inches on the news pages of Monday's papers, accompanied by lurid photographs of battered Brivois not fit for viewing before the watershed. One witness described blood on the floor with bottles, chairs and glasses flying through the air. The fight between the rival supporters seems to have sucked in about sixty people, players included. The Pontypridd side maintained the fight had started when one of them was hit by a flying bottle. The contestants in the other corner insisted Ponty had come in at 10.30 and, in revenge for losing, attacked the far-from-soft Philippe Carbonneau, the Brive scrum-half who'd been involved in Mcintosh's dismissal. A couple of elderly local gendarmes arrived to view the contest, wisely decided they were not match fit and summoned the A team to lob in some tear gas to signal full-time.

Lamaison and Carbonneau both had their noses broken, and Venditti's eyes were as black as plums next day. 'They smashed everything. I have never seen anything so violent in all my life,' Lamaison told a reporter. 'It was like being in a Western. We've been through a real nightmare.' Even the tough Carbonneau admitted that 'before the police came we were really afraid.' The following day Mcintosh, hooker Phil John and Ponty's South African centre, Andre Barnard, were all arrested and, although allowed to return to Wales, were warned that they could face a two-year prison stretch. Brive demanded a life ban for the three players and the expulsion of Pontypridd from the European Cup. The organisers refused both proposals, and apportioned blame – at least for events on the pitch, which was as far as they could pass sentence – equally, fining each side £15,000, with a further suspended fine of the same amount. After that decision, the Ponty treasurers were not so much rubbing their hands as wringing them.

But if Pontypridd were rightly blamed for the disgrace of Le Toulzac, many players and observers remain baffled by the extraordinarily split personality of French club rugby. The French can play like angels or like devils, with clean-cut flair or with savage thuggery, sometimes within the same match. Poland's Gregory Kacala played at Brive: 'One minute it is quiet on the field. Then, boom. It all goes crazy, completely crazy.' That can bring out the beast in others, as it brought out the beast in Pontypridd on that infamous day. It's fair to conclude that, as far as the rugby was concerned, both teams should have been red with shame.

Slammed Out

Wales v England, Wembley, April 1999

After 89 years it had all come down to this – the last match of the last Five Nations tournament before Italy joined the circus to kick off both a new millennium and the Six Nations. Incongruously, it was being played at Wembley, the twentieth century's home of soccer. 'Few championships,' wrote David Hands in *The Times*, 'have matched the roller-coaster ride of this one,' so things were beautifully set up for that final match between Wales and England, with England all set for another Grand Slam. 'Sport does not come much better, nor embrace so many twists and turns,' said Hands after it was all over. And indeed the game had everything except, from a purely English perspective, the right result.

Within three minutes, Dan Luger had gone coasting in for a converted try to put England 7–0 ahead, maybe giving them a false sense of superiority and unquestionably providing them with a lead they were to preserve for a further 79 minutes. Midway through the first half, nineteen-year-old Steve Hanley touched down for try number two, and on the stroke of half-time Richard Hill pounced on a Welsh error to force himself in for a third. In between times, that indefatigable goal-kicker, Neil Jenkins, kept punishing English infringements. Six penalties were put away to keep Wales in touch at the interval, 25–18. They were penalties England were to regret, though with less soul-searching than two critical clangers that were to come later.

Invigorated by their half-time tonic water, or whatever the healthy young bucks of modern rugby are required to pour down themselves these days, England trotted back onto Wembley's broad acres for their final forty minutes on the path to another Grand Slam. Almost directly from the restart Neil Back, in his own 22 and under no pressure at all, stooped to gather a rolling ball and knocked on horribly. The resulting scrum paved the way for Wales's first try of the game, scored by Shane Howarth, who it subsequently transpired did not have genuine valley blood coursing through his veins. Jenkins converted – of course. In the first half, as Gerald Davies was quick to point out afterwards, Jonny Wilkinson, Hanley, Luger and Mike Catt had all broken clear of the Welsh defence, if not at will, then certainly often enough to have had much more than a slender seven-point advantage at the interval. Instead, the score was now tied at 25–25 and Wales had taken heart in what should have been a thankless situation for them.

Nevertheless, as the countdown to the final whistle started, England had hauled themselves back into the lead with two Wilkinson penalties, and tightened their own game sufficiently to ensure Neil Jenkins had no further kickable opportunities. It was 31–25 when, in the 76th minute, England made their second fatal blunder. Winning a penalty within range of Wilkinson's reliable boot, England skipper Lawrence Dallaglio ordered the kick to be put into the corner for an England lineout. Instead of finding themselves nine points adrift and requiring two scores to retrieve the match with only minutes remaining, Wales had been thrown a lifeline. They not only saved their own lives, but proceeded to turn England's to ashes. England held out into injury time but, ninety seconds in, Wales had a lineout. Chris Wyatt rose to tap it down and set Scott Quinnell away on one of his beefy, barrelling charges into midfield. Scott Gibbs hit the pass hard and straight and, recalling memories of his Lions glory days, tore past four flailing defenders in a passable impression of an Exocet missile. One point in it, with Neil Jenkins eyeing up the posts as he prepared for the conversion. After all the pressure kicks he's put away in his career, Jenkins was never going to miss this one. The only wager worth making was whether he would kick it within an inch of dead centre. He did, and Wales had torpedoed England at the death, 32–31. 'That the game should have arrived at such a climax was, in large part, England's own doing,' said Gerald Davies. 'It was a failure of their own making.' Commented Michael Lynagh: 'England must be a shattered unit after this defeat.' Not shattered – they continued to play some glorious rugby in the next three years – but less certain, perhaps. In 2000, they again stumbled with the Slam in their grasp, this time against Scotland. In 2001, they travelled to Dublin, admittedly after a six-month postponement caused by the foot-and-mouth crisis, and fluffed their Grand Slam lines again.

De Beer Drops in to Spoil the Party

England v South Africa, World Cup quarter-final, 1999

England fans look back to their quarter-final defeat at the hands of the Springboks in the 1999 World Cup with particular disappointment. Although they knew the England squad was in the early days of redevelopment and could not hope to lift the Cup, they did expect at least to reach the semi-finals. As it was, Jannie de Beer slotted no fewer than five second-half dropped goals in the space of just eighteen minutes to send the sweet charioteers swinging low and out of the competition. Almost to a man and woman, the press and the public thought England had choked on the big occasion. But there is another side to the story.

De Beer's dropped goals were not the sparks of sudden inspiration that everyone assumed, but carefully preplanned. The Springboks noticed that, under their new defence coach, Phil Larder, England were using a Rugby League form of drift defence. This meant that when the opposing backs attempted a break, the attacker was likely to be hit by two, possibly three, tacklers – but it also suggested the fly-half had a fraction more time to play with. De Beer studied videos of England's games in the tournament's pool stages, and concluded he would have a few seconds more than usual – enough time to get in a drop kick. 'If I'd scored a couple in the first half,' de Beer said later, 'England would have had the interval to work out a counter.' As it was, he was never in the right position for an attempt at goal until the second half. Then, 'by the time England had worked out it was a planned move I'd got five in eighteen minutes. No team can recover from that.' England certainly couldn't. They lost 44–21, and were left once more to dream of the next World Cup.

'The Only Explanation is That We Are French'

France v New Zealand, World Cup semi-final, 1999

France entered the 1999 World Cup as holders of the wooden spoon in the Five Nations and on the back of their worst run of results for thirty years. If all went as anticipated in the seedings, they would come up against the All Blacks in the semi-finals, to whom they had lost by 54–7 in Wellington only four months earlier. Drawn in the weakest of the pools, France's progress had been shaky, to say the least, and by their own admission they had put together barely ten minutes of decent rugby in the process, sinking to real awfulness in grinding out a shaky 47–13 win over Namibia. Against Fiji they seemed certain to take French leave until a final rally enabled them to squeeze home 28–19, and only then after referee Pat O'Brien had disallowed a first-half Fijian try that the replays showed to be copper-bottomed.

New Zealand, by contrast, were the clear favourites to stroll through to the Final, where they might possibly be required to raise a gentle sweat to defeat either the Wallabies or the Springboks before ambling away with the Cup. They went through the pool matches like a battleship, armoured at every point and with formidable firepower when they chose to train their guns.

Never has the form book been so thoroughly confounded. 'One of the greatest reverses rugby union has seen in its entire history,' proclaimed *The Times* gleefully. 'A French triumph that ranks as one of the greatest upsets in sport,' concluded Simon Barnes. Here was a classic clash between fifteen chokers and fifteen jokers, and the jokers had triumphed. What had gone wrong?

At the interval, all seemed to be running to expectation. The All Blacks led 17–10 thanks to an unconverted try by Jonah Lomu, the personification of the Kiwi battleship, and four precision penalties from Andrew Mehrtens, against a single penalty and a converted try, all the French points coming from fly-half Christophe Lamaison. The only straw in the wind had been the nature of the French try, which had come from Christophe Dominici, who 'launched a demented run' through the New Zealand defence to put Lamaison over. At the time, it seemed like a small but florid piece of icing on the All Black cake, and the impression was heightened five minutes after the restart, when Lomu crossed for his second try to increase New Zealand's lead to 24–10.

Instead, with the Twickenham crowd roaring them passionately on, it was the spark that lit a French blaze of 33 points in 27 minutes, and the guy on top of the bonfire was wearing the silver fern. Skipper Raphael Ibanez said afterwards: 'I can't explain what happened. The only explanation is that we are French.' First, Lamaison dropped two goals in two minutes to narrow the deficit to 24–16. Then he slotted two penalties as the Blacks began to make mistakes under pressure. It was 24–22 now, and Lamaison had scored every one of the French points. It was at this point that Kiwi fullback Jeff Wilson had what David Hands called 'a moment of madness'. With ball in hand, instead of running left to enter the comfort zone of having man-mountain Lomu alongside him, he checked, turned and ran straight into the French pack. He lost the ball, and scrum-half Fabien Galthie kicked for Dominici on the wing to gather and run forty metres for the second French try, which, naturally, Lamaison converted. Four more minutes, and Richard Dourthe went cruising over to make it 36–24. The French seemed to gather their breath for a quarter of an hour before Philippe Bernat-Salles brought the crowd to its feet once more with his celebrated impression of a silver-tailed firework as he flew over for try number four. Yet again, Lamaison converted immaculately.

Never before had New Zealand conceded 43 points in an international and, although a last-minute try from Jeff Wilson salvaged a sliver of comfort, the 43–31 defeat was as shocking a sporting reverse as the All Blacks had ever experienced. Said skipper Taine Randell, 'We didn't try to shut up shop. We didn't underestimate them. They just outplayed us.' As for the French, Simon Barnes hit the nail on the head: 'They played as if they had never known anything except brilliance, their recent past of fumbling mediocrity and confused game plans a figment of somebody else's imagination.' Learning from New Zealand's mistake, the Wallabies did shut up shop, defensively speaking, in the Final one week later. France couldn't light the blaze a second time, and Australia lifted the World Cup.

The Plank That Turned into a Springboard

Australia v British & Irish Lions, second and third Tests, 2001

The Lions had never lost a series against Australia and when, two minutes and 48 seconds into the first Test, Jason Robinson shredded the Wallaby defence to score a thrilling try as a prelude to a spectacular victory, the chances of retaining the record seemed high. In the end the Lions, or what was left of the pride as injuries piled one on top of another, were to be disappointed, but where, in the second and third Tests, did it all go wrong? In retrospect, there were probably three turning points – two, both in the second Test, which opened the way to Australian triumph, and a third at the very death that could have saved the tour.

The first-Test hammering had sent shock waves through the Wallaby camp. A team whose style of playing they thought they knew, and had accordingly underrated, had outplayed Australia at its own style of rugby. Predictably, the first half of the second Test was a ferocious battle for supremacy, but one the Lions seemed to be winning as they led 17–3 a little before half-time. Richard Hill had been the outstanding forward of the series when his tour was abruptly ended by Nathan Grey, whose trailing arm caught him on the head, off the ball, and poleaxed him. Whether it was deliberate or not, whether it was elbow or upper arm, no amount of subsequent video study could determine, but the effect of Hill's loss was immediately noticeable. The supreme George Gregan now had those vital seconds more, and therefore greater space, in which to play.

No sooner had the second half started than Jonny Wilkinson made a mistake. As Eddie Butler noted, 'this is not a sentence that will be written often in the history of rugby,' but it was a mistake that seemed, both at the time and in retrospect, to have turned the match. Wilkinson had the ball in hand on his own 22 when, with the best of attacking notions, he opted to float a pass to his wing. The decision was too slow and the execution too deliberate. If those watching could see it coming, Joe Roff down at ground level certainly could as he intercepted and was off into the corner. Although it took a video replay to confirm the try was good, Roff and the Wallabies had no doubts, and the scores were level. Within minutes, Matt Burke had landed a penalty, and Roff a second try, as the Lions' concentration faltered, and within ten minutes of the restart, the series was effectively all square. Roll on the decider.

Austin Healey is not a man to whom you can be indifferent, and Justin Harrison belongs to that section of humanity that can't stand him. They had already had a little spat when Australia A beat the Lions in Gosford, and carefully turned the spat into a feud when the Lions' midweek dirt-trackers snatched a last-gasp victory against the ACT Brumbies. Harrison was brought into the Australian side for the final Test. Healey was down to play and allowed it to emerge in his ghosted newspaper column that he did not think highly of Justin. The words 'ape', 'plod' and 'plank' featured in the article alongside some unflattering views of Australian manhood in general because, as Austin subsequently explained, if it provoked the opposition to come gunning for him they wouldn't be playing good rugby. A clever little joke that might have worked, had he not had to withdraw from the side with a bulging disc, leaving Harrison free to concentrate on his rugby and make the joke backfire.

The third Test, possibly the biggest rugby match of all time, swayed agonisingly back and forth in front of 84,000 spectators and, as the final quarter began, appeared locked at 23–23. Was it possible it would all end in a draw, even though the Lions seemed imprisoned in their own half? It was not. Two penalties gave the Wallabies a six-point lead as the countdown to the hooter began. Then a Lions penalty enabled Wilkinson to kick – perfectly – for the corner. A catch, a forward drive, a touchdown and another miracle conversion by Jonny would bring a one-point victory in the last minute. Keith Wood threw to Martin Johnson – and from somewhere all six feet eight inches of Justin Harrison, the 'plank', sprang across the Lions' skipper, claimed the ball and Campo's catastrophe of 1989 was avenged (see page 112).

It's Time to Make Crossbars Bigger

Llanelli's assault on the Heineken European Cup, 2000, 2001 & 2002

You don't have to be Welsh to find Llanelli's bad luck in the European Cup in the early 2000s well-nigh unbearable. Stop giggling up there in the East Midlands, not to mention Gloucester. You were lucky, and you know it. When Northampton's Mr Reliable, Paul Grayson, landed a penalty in the dying seconds of the semi-final of the 2000 Cup to deny Llanelli a place in the final against Munster – a final Northampton went on to win – it seemed nothing too far out of the ordinary. Plenty of games are won or lost in the dying moments, and learning to accept the dashed cup is all part of life's rich tapestry. But three such hammer blows on the trot is another matter altogether. Could it be that God is not a Welshman after all? Could it be that Gareth, Barry, JPR, Cliff, Phil and Ieuan are not his disciples on earth, and that Max Boyce's Epistles are not divinely inspired? Shocking questions but, as the 2001 and 2002 seasons wore on, the thought must have hammered at the back of the collective Llanelli mind with increasing urgency.

Pool Five of the 2001 Cup put Llanelli in the same group as Gloucester. Their away leg against Gloucester was their fifth fixture in the pool and they were two points ahead of the West-Countrymen. It was a critical match, in which victory would see them virtually assured of a place in the quarter-finals and, unsurprisingly, it was a 'raucous, drama-filled encounter in front of 10,800 at Kingsholm.' Gloucester had played poorly. They were slow and bereft of ideas, whereas Llanelli had played better, try-scoring rugby, and had led throughout the game. As the game entered its final minute, the despairing roars from the Shed virtually blew the home team upfield, still trailing 25–27, for one last assault. From a ruck virtually under the Llanelli posts, the ball came back to Elton Moncrieff, the Gloucester scrum-half, who snatched at an attempted dropped goal.

It was a horrible effort, and he must have cursed as the ball slid off his boot low across the backs of his stooping forwards. Phil Booth, Llanelli's amply built prop, was just easing his aching body from the ruck when the ball met his rounded form and, deflecting from the curved surface, looped upwards just enough to clear the bar and flop down the other side. It was an outrageous fluke and rank injustice, but it had happened. Llanelli were out of the 2001 Heineken Cup at the pool stage, and the coach trip back to the valleys that evening was a sombre affair.

Lady Luck appeared to be riding shotgun in Llanelli's 2002 European Cup campaign, however. England's champions, Leicester, were twice beaten in the pool matches, but both progressed to the quarter-finals, and then found themselves drawn against each other in the semi-finals. Llanelli seemed to have the measure of Leicester and this time, surely, there would be no mistakes. Llanelli did, indeed, have the best of the first half or, maybe, one might say Leicester had the worst of it. They played poorly, but perhaps this was the Llanelli effect. They were simply not allowed to play well. Leicester's second-half effort, though, was greatly improved as they sought to play a positive, creative game. They dominated play, but without the ability to control the ball in the tackle and this cost them the opportunity, except on one occasion, to cross the try line.

Once again, Llanelli led right up to the last minute of full-time, just as they had against Northampton and Gloucester, and this time it really did look as if Leicester's best efforts had foundered on Llanelli's defence. They had managed to keep play inside the Leicester half, and then it happened. Llanelli were penalised for collapsing a scrum and, from 58 metres out and inside the touchline, Tim Stimpson stepped up to kick. Skipper Martin Johnson made it plain that it was Stimpson's decision to go for goal, not his. 'It was a question of head down, don't try to hit it too hard, and let the technique work for you,' Stimpson said. From such a range, the ball seemed to take an eternity before it began its descent. It landed on the crossbar, bounced up, hit the inside of the post, and fell over on the Llanelli side to give Leicester a 13–12 win. 'The width of a crossbar, no more, separated Llanelli from the place they and the country crave,' wrote David Hands in *The Times*.

Van Zyl Blackens the Name of Springbok Rugby

South Africa v New Zealand, Tri-Nations, Durban, August 2002

Saturday 10 August 2002 – a day to live in rugby's Hall of Infamy. There had been nothing to suggest this would be the case, even if the first half of this fast and thrilling Tri-Nations game between the Springboks and the All Blacks had had its contentious moments. Within two minutes of the start, the Boks had scored a converted try, only for the All Blacks to storm straight up the other end and grab five points back. Shortly after, referee David McHugh awarded the Blacks a slightly harsh penalty try; and then compounded a sense of injustice in the South African crowd by disallowing an elegant try from Springbok Brenton Paulse with a somewhat debatable obstruction ruling against James Dalton. Nevertheless, the game flowed excitingly, if sometimes raggedly, from end to end until striking half-time parity at seventeen points each.

The second half was only a few minutes old, and referee McHugh was setting a scrum inside the Springbok half with his back to the touchline, when an overweight 42-year-old called Pieter van Zyl, with more flab than muscle and an excess of either over brainpower, wobbled out of the crowd and onto the field. With all the courage of the self-righteous, he attacked McHugh from behind, wrestling him to the ground before the forwards of both sides realised what was happening. The opposing flankers, Richie McCaw and A J Venter, promptly formed a maul to dispose of the intruder.

McHugh left the field on a golf cart with what appeared to be a broken arm, but turned out to be a dislocated shoulder and, after a ten-minute break, Chris White took over as referee. The All Blacks won 30–23, a result that mattered only to the most partisan. The managing director of South Africa Rugby said afterwards: 'We'll make sure van Zyl never attends a rugby match in South Africa again.' Or anywhere else, one hopes. If English soccer fans can lose their passports for their behaviour off the pitch, the same fate seems the least that van Zyl should suffer. It's difficult to imagine anything worse than rugby followers, traditionally welcoming and fair-minded, being tarred with the reputation of such a shameful character.

Eight into Six Won't Go – Not Even if They're All Blacks

New Zealand v England, July 2003

Clive Woodward knew he had to risk it. It was all very well beating the All Blacks at Twickenham, but if England had serious aspirations to win the World Cup down under, he had to take his team to New Zealand and win there. No matter that Johnno, Wilko and the rest had just finished a long and strenuous season. Irrelevant that England had landed that elusive Grand Slam only weeks before. The time to rest would come in July, after matches against the Blacks and the Wallabies that were to test their mettle and forge it in southern hemisphere fire.

In the event, 'England scored a narrow victory on the field,' as Mick Clearly put it, 'and a landmark triumph in the mind.' John Mitchell admitted as much at the press conference after the game: 'England will gain a lot mentally from this victory,' he said. It was irrelevant that the All Blacks scored the only try of the game and irrelevant that Wilkinson had one of his poorest games in a white shirt (despite scoring all of England's points – four penalties and a dropped goal). The fact remained that England played badly and won 15–13 in the All Blacks' Wellington citadel.

The game turned on ten minutes shortly into the second half. The Blacks laid siege to the England line, and referee Stuart Dickinson quite correctly sent both Neil Back and Lawrence Dallaglio to the sin bin for professional fouls and awarded a penalty against England. Thus was born the Goal-line Stand that has already entered the mythology of rugby. The All Blacks could have opted to kick the penalty and taken three assured points, knowing that nine minutes remained for camping on the English line. But they reckoned a minimum of one try was there for the taking, and it was that arrogance that cost them the match. Loose-head prop Graham Rowntree, one of the six heroes left to take on the eight of New Zealand, said afterwards, 'The All Blacks were telling us they'd have us.' It's no good talking a good game, though; you have to perform it. The scrum went down, and it went down again, and again and yet again. The six men of England gave not an inch. 'What was going through your head?' the reporters asked Martin Johnson afterwards. 'My spine,' came the reply. Johnno would have enjoyed that little exchange. 'Well what were you telling the rest of the guys?' they persisted, desperate for quotes of a Churchillian or Shakespearean hue. 'I told them to bend over and push,' came the reply, eloquent in its deadpan certainty.

And push they did, but not just push. Despite two of their back row being off the field, they still contrived to police the fringes, knocking back scrum-half Justin Marshall and No 8 Rodney So'oialo as they probed for the line. Richard Hill, who always does the work of two men, took on the mantle of three. The whole team – or the thirteen that were left – played as if their rugby lives depended upon it, and they held out. There was once an old truth about England being a bunch of Public School Poms. The Kiwis probably still believed it. The Goal-line Stand, indeed the whole 80 minutes that contained it, taught them something beyond all previous experience of the wearers of the Red Rose.

Watson Today's Menu – Stuffed Ham?

The World Cup, November 2003

We can all agree that Australia hosted the 2003 World Cup brilliantly. They organise big events well down under, and not the least of their triumphs was the marketing of the Pool A tie between Namibia and Romania in Launceston, Tasmania. A full stadium and a cheerful, buzzing crowd for a tie that might have been considered an unfashionable turn-off in other circumstances. There were black spots, nevertheless. Italy and Argentina have every right to feel aggrieved by the way the IRB gave them so little recovery time between matches. And the standard of a few of the southern hemisphere referees verged on the disgraceful. Two of them, in particular, had gone way past their sell-by dates.

In Pool D the All Blacks were being given the shock of their lives by a fiery, creative Welsh side who were punching repeated holes in their opponents' midfield and took a 37–24 lead five minutes into the second half. The Blacks came back with two converted tries to edge back in front 38–37 when South Africa's Andre Watson dropped a real clanger. Doug Howlett took a pass – let's call it that for the moment – from Justin Marshall and scored in the corner. There was a slight problem. Marshall's pass was so far forward, a lesser man than Howlett would have needed a taxi to catch it. Did Mr Watson give Wales a scrum? He did not. Instead he called for the video referee to take a look and see if Howlett's foot was in touch. 'The pass was good,' he told the video ref, not once but twice, as viewers of the large screen in the stadium and on TV at home looked on disbelievingly at repeat performances of a pass that would have done credit to an American quarter-back. The Blacks might well have won without Mr Watson's able assistance, but that try was the nail in Wales's coffin.

Next on the distasteful menu was the dreadful display of New Zealand's Steve Walsh. He was put in charge, if that's not too strong an expression, of the Australia–Scotland Pool B game, and his subsequent performance was a strong contender for the scandal of the World Cup. Australia were giving a somewhat less than convincing performance and the Scots, for once in the tournament, were playing with a degree of conviction when, in the first half, there occurred a moment 'when the sequence of events defied belief,' as Mark Reason reported. The Wallabies ex-Rugby League wing, Wendell Sailor, was adding to his catalogue of unimpressive games when, under no pressure, he knocked on in midfield. Feeling as silly as he looked, he decided to flatten someone, and as Scottish second row Nathan Hines was handy at the time, he felt the full force of Wendell's self-reproach. The loose ball, meantime, was enthusiastically seized by Kenny Logan, who, seeing an open path to the line, set off at full throttle. He was halfway there when Mr Walsh, remembering where he lived, belatedly blew for a penalty – a penalty to Scotland, certainly, but a nice safe penalty in the middle of the field. Even supposing Scotland could kick it from there (they couldn't), three points was less damaging than the seven that had been on offer. Scotland were furious, but could at least contemplate the next ten minutes with only fourteen Australians on the field. Not a hope. Mr Walsh did raise the energy to wag a finger at Sailor, but of a yellow card (never mind a red) there was no glimmer.

Had this been an isolated decision, and had the refereeing been otherwise even-handed, it would have been unfortunate. But it was simply the most spectacular in a series of inept decisions. Let us pass over the regularity with which Australia sent decoy runners across the path of the ball-carrier to take out the opposition without incurring a single oscillation of the Walsh digit, still less the penalty decreed in the Laws. Let us instead consider the critical moment in the second half when, with the scores tied, the Wallaby flanker, Phil Waugh, turned the ball over for his side, and Australia scored. 'It would be stretching the bounds of geometry,' said Reason, 'to say that Waugh came in from the side of the maul, so far offside was he.' Or the moment later in the half when Stephen Larkham tried a speculative, long-range drop at the Scottish posts. The ball hit the bar, the Scots went to gather it and there was second-row Justin Harrison, at least twenty metres offside, obstructing Scotland's attempts to clear to such effect that they could only scramble the ball towards touch for the Wallabies to gather, attack and win the penalty that should have been – but wasn't – given the other way a moment earlier. And so it went on. And on.

Which brings us back to Andre Watson, and the Final between Australia and England. He gave another display that could be called inexplicable but for his well-known distaste (just ask the French) for anything as nasty and brutish as a scrum. So long as both packs are quiet and refined in the set piece, and one does not cause the other any discomfort by, for example, putting the squeeze on, Andre can sometimes restrain himself. This, though, was the World Cup Final, and so prestigious a contest needed someone capable of understanding that it is not the referee's job to ensure spectacle and entertainment as though it were a game of basketball, but to officiate to the laws of the game of rugby, a hard, physical game in which winning possession is crucial. Within minutes of the start, 'Australia's scrum was,' as Stephen Jones reported in the *Sunday Times*, 'in desperate straits.' It was thought beforehand that Al Baxter, the Wallaby tight-head, might prove a weak link, and so it transpired. 'England proceeded to drive Australia back at will.' Yet Watson penalised the English scrum (which had not, until this game, incurred a single scrummaging penalty throughout the tournament) six times. Why? Does a dominant scrum *need* to infringe? 'What were you playing at, Andre Watson?' demanded ex-Welsh international Eddie Butler in *The Observer*. 'An appalling match,' said Welshman Stephen Jones of his performance. 'An utter disgrace,' said Irishman Mick Cleary in *The Daily Telegraph*.

Watson reserved his pièce de résistance for the last minute of full-time, with England deservedly three points clear. Martin Johnson was illegally – and blatantly – hauled down at a lineout near the English line. It should have been a penalty, a relieving kick to touch and a throw in to England, who would have kept possession until the whistle blew. The offence went unremarked by Watson in favour of an England knock-on as the lineout disengaged. A scrum to Australia and, even as the front rows engaged, Watson blew for a penalty against Trevor Woodman. The ostensible reason was for not engaging at the right angle. 'The thought formed,' Eddie Butler wrote, 'that this was nothing better than guesswork on the part of the official.' Maybe. The speed with which he blew led to the conclusion that the penalty against England was premeditated possibly, thought one commentator, in retribution for a remark made earlier by Woodman. Australia landed the penalty – a magnificent pressure kick from the touchline by Elton Flatley – and the game went to extra time. England won, but had they not Andre Watson's refereeing would, as Stephen Jones said, 'have been the primary scandal of the sporting year.'

Dominici Takes French Leave

**France v Italy; Scotland v England, Six Nations,
February 2004**

Christophe Dominici is one of the most elusive wingers and exciting runners that even France has produced, and he was probably looking forward to adding to his 16 international tries as he ran out against Italy, the current holders of the Six Nations wooden spoon. Italy were showing signs of improvement under their Kiwi coach, John Kirwan, but only six days earlier had suffered a brutal afternoon in Rome against world champions England, going down 9–50. So Dominici had every reason to suppose he could add to his try tally in front of his own adoring crowd in the Stade de France.

France had one of their unimpressive days. Maybe they thought they only had to run onto the pitch to win; maybe Italy's fierce defence and never-say-die pack jolted them out of their stride. At half-time, they led by a less than convincing 13–0, and although the crowd weren't whistling yet, one sensed Gallic disapproval might not be far away. And then, eleven minutes into the second half, France got the inspiration they wanted. From 45 metres out, Dominici saw half a gap in the Italian defence, and broke clean through. Only the fullback stood between him and a try under the posts, and when can you ever recall Dominici failing in such a situation? He flew past the hapless defender and crossed the line to the immediate left of the posts. But he just could not resist one last little moment of showboating. Instead of plonking the ball down, he curved gracefully inwards, round behind the posts and on nearly to the dead-ball line, holding the ball casually in one hand as the other got ready to receive the crowd's acclaim. And dropped it! Yes, folks, he dropped it over the dead-ball line, and the Italians had a five-metre scrum. Did he feel embarrassed? You bet he did. Did the crowd start whistling? They certainly did. France won, 25–0, but far from convincingly, and Dominici never did get on the score sheet.

It wasn't the only hilarious incident that day. Over at Murrayfield, Scotland and England were engaged in bashing each other around in traditional manner for the Calcutta Cup. England were comfortably ahead when, around the 62nd minute, Scotland's No 8, Simon Taylor, went to the sin bin for a professional foul. The English pack licked its lips and prepared to bludgeon the remaining seven members of their Scottish counterparts. Sure enough, in the 68th minute it began a massive rumble towards the line. Over the 22 it trundled, gathering the momentum of a steamroller, on and on towards the line. 'Oh, here we go,' said Eddie Butler in the commentary box, 'it's a try, it's a try.' It wasn't. The bulldozer ground remorselessly onwards, and crashed straight into the left-hand post. The ball carrier, Lawrence Dallaglio, was jerked upwards, the Scots wrenched the ball from him and wrestled it away to safety. England won, 35–13, but it was good to see human frailty back on the agenda.

Mutiny in the Hive – Bees Oust Wasps

Pertemps Bees v Wasps, Powergen Cup quarter-final, 2004

When the quarter-final draw for the 2004 Powergen Cup was made and Wasps were told they were playing Pertemps Bees, quite a buzz arose in the nest. It wasn't that they felt impelled to sharpen their stings, more that they weren't quite sure what Pertemps Bees was. A health supplement that had escaped the EU ban perhaps? One of those little drinkies full of friendly bacteria? But thanks to the miracle of modern science and internet search engines, they soon discovered that this was a cunning nom de plume for First Division side Birmingham Solihull. So that was all right. No problems to be expected there. The buzzing in the nest dropped to a gentle whisper and the Wasps went back to sleep. Come the day, all they had to do was rest the soldiers and send out a few of the drones to do the business and the impertinent Bees would be sorry they'd left the hive.

In the very best tradition of cup ties, the Premiership champions crept back to the nest a sadder and sorrier group of insects as part-timers Birmingham Solihull (or Pertemps Bees, if you must) put it across them 24–28 at the Causeway Stadium, High Wycombe. It was not by any means the first great upset in cup history, but it was the first since the age of professionalism dawned. As such, it gave hope to those who play rugby more for love than money from one end of the country to the other. As the press reported the following day, Wasps 'were out-thought and out-fought' by Solihull. It didn't seem likely when, in a quarter of an hour of the first half, Wasps flew in for three tries, two of them gifted by some naive defending. But Solihull re-grouped and put such pressure on the Wasps pack that they denied them both ball and space. Better still, the pressure forced Wasps into giving away penalties, six of which electrician and

Saturday fly-half Mark Woodrow happily converted. Solihull were not content to rely on opposition mistakes for their points, though. Either side of half-time they created two good tries of their own. The second came from a clever little chip that Woodrow floated into the path of Kiwi Aaron Takarangi, who had been about to fly home for the funeral of his father-in-law, but delayed his departure to play.

When Cardiff were dumped out of the SWALEC Cup in 1993 by St Peter's, their Aussie coach had been sullen and ungracious (see page 58). Wasps' director of rugby, New Zealander Warren Gatland, is cut from more sporting cloth. He saw no need to complain about the referee, the linesmen, the conditions or even the conjunction of the planets, but praised Solihull and accepted the blame for underestimating his opponents. His Solihull opposite number, Phil Maynard, said: 'The Premiership clubs keep trying to shut us out, particularly financially, but perhaps this will have opened a few people's eyes.' He thought for a moment before adding, 'Then again, we might have made the situation worse!' Looking at the way Rotherham were so ruthlessly denied their rightful place in the Premiership in 2002, he might just be right.

'It Is Time to Panic'

All Blacks v The Lions, Christchurch, June 2005

As the All Blacks performed the haka, supposedly traditional but actually an invention for the purposes of rugby, you could have forgiven Brian O'Driscoll, the Lions' captain (for precisely 90 seconds as it was to turn out) if he had spent the time introducing his players to one another. It was the first time they had played together as a unit, yet here they were about to face the Blacks at home – probably the stiffest examination that any Lion can expect to undergo. The first mistake on this ill-fated tour was the size of the touring party – so large that the handful of qualified players left at home must have felt lonely and unloved with so many of their mates down under. Perhaps unsurprisingly in these circumstances the warm-up games had not gone well as different combinations were tried and players who, in former days, would not even have been on the tour, had to be given a run-out. It's all very well having every position and eventuality covered in triplicate but not much help if, metaphorically speaking, they all keep running around getting in each other's way and obscuring the manager's view of the bigger picture. As a result, it seemed, the Lions had lost or narrowly hung on to that which they ought to have won with ease and worse, by the eve of the first of the three Tests, it was still unclear which players would work well alongside others.

Clive Woodward solved the problem by ignoring the current form of individuals such as Gavin Henson and packing his Lions team with ageing Englishmen reckoning, it seemed, that length of tooth would compensate for blunted claws. Yes, England had achieved a heroic triumph in the World Cup, but that was two years earlier and the game and its tactics had continued to change in the intervening period. The preceding northern hemisphere season had made it abundantly clear that England had failed to keep abreast of such changes, whereas Wales had stormed adventurously to a Grand

Slam and the Six Nations title. Even so, Sir Clive trusted only four Welshmen to start against the All Blacks.

The game was ninety seconds old when All Black skipper, Tana Umaga, and hooker Keven Mealamu each grabbed a leg of Brian O'Driscoll, upended him and bopped him into the turf head first, the ball, the action and the referee being elsewhere at the time. O'Driscoll played no more rugby in 2005, but it goes without saying that New Zealand officials saw nothing wrong in any of this, pursuing their long-established tradition (see page 121) that anything is permissible so long as a fellow New Zealander is not on the receiving end. It was a nasty beginning and robbed the Lions of their most incisive runner, but it made no difference to the outcome of the match since, as became ever more apparent, his side could not win the possession that might have delivered the ball to O'Driscoll in any case.

The assumption before the match was that the Lions had the stronger pack, whereas the All Blacks, brilliant runners behind the scrum as everyone acknowledged them to be, were flaky up front. When the rain poured down before and during the game everyone expected a good, old-fashioned 'stuff it up the jumper and grind to the line' approach from the visitors. In the event 'those New Zealand forwards refused to get in touch with their feminine side,' as Michael Aylwin deftly put it in the *Observer*. Bluntly stated, they dominated every exchange and in particular the lineout, with ten takes on the Lions' throw. As Eddie Butler wrote, 'from the very first throw it was clear the basic set-piece was a shambles. On at least three occasions the Lions failed to get a single jumper into the air.' By the end of one of the most dispiriting performances a Lions supporter could dread seeing, the one puzzle was that the All Blacks scored only two tries and won by a margin, 21–3, that barely hinted at the scale of the massacre. Perhaps Austin Healey put his finger on it when he said 'If it hadn't been raining, it would have been a 40-pointer ... It is time to panic. If he (Woodward) doesn't make changes, the tour is heading down the pan.' But faced with back-to-back Tests, the damage had been done. Despite the changes, the Lions went down 48–18 in the second Test, 38–19 in the third and couldn't wait to get home and wake to find the 'Long Black Night' had all been a bad dream.

A Trial Run for the World Cup?

England's tour of New Zealand, June 2008

Forty years or so ago touring rugby sides whiled away the dark evenings of inactivity by trashing the fixtures and furnishings of whichever hotel they happened to be in (see page 76). How charmingly quaint this seems in the professional twenty-first-century era. Nowadays, in the gaps between World Cup years, northern hemisphere sides are in and out of southern hemisphere countries like yoyos, seeking to measure themselves in advance of the next big showdown. On the rugby field, England's 2008 visit to All Black territory was not a success, singularly failing to live up to the famous victory of July 2003 (see page 152). The two-Test series finished 37–20 and 44–12 to the Blacks with a try count of nine to four in their favour.

But let's look on the bright side. Even if there's only a week between the two Tests there's still time for after-hours shenanigans – isn't there? If reports at the time were to be believed, Mike Brown, Topsy Ojo, Danny Care and David Strettle reckoned there was. Ever alert for a whiff of scandal, the journalistic hacks who loiter on the fringes of touring sports teams had a story in almost no time. It 'emerged' that the foursome had 'sexually violated an 18 year-old woman in the team hotel.' Evidently there had been no safety for her in numbers. But was it true? The Auckland police arrived on the scene, and His Honour Judge Jeff Blackett was called in to investigate, pronounce and, as necessary, the RFU would punish.

A problem arose almost at once. The woman in question submitted a written statement but refused to be cross-examined in person or by video. Her statement admitted she had agreed to go to the room of one of the players (Mike Brown, as it turned out) and that 'there was consensual activity', but that three other players then entered the room, at which point there was 'non-consensual activity'. Or, in plainer language, an agreed romp in the hay turned into rape. Witnesses, however, stated that on leaving the woman 'did not seem to be distressed' and the judge was not able to see her medical records. She also issued a statement saying that she would not be taking the matter further (i.e. selling her story to the press) and would leave people to make up their own minds.

So what did happen? Auckland police ruled Strettle out of their enquiries as he was evidently otherwise engaged that night with a different and uncomplaining woman. (She sold her story to a newspaper, and he was warned about his future conduct.) Ojo and Brown, it seemed, had met the young woman at the centre of the story in a bar where Ojo admitted kissing her, and they had gone off to a nightclub, she and Brown returning to his hotel room at 7.30 in the morning. Just as well there wasn't a match on the immediate horizon. Ojo meanwhile was due for a session with the physiotherapist at 8.15, after which he went to Brown's room while the latter went off for a similar session. Shortly thereafter, Strettle and Care put their heads round the door to remind Ojo he had a pool session at 9.00. For the avoidance of all doubt it should be stated that Danny Care had been having an early night, as a good rugby player should, turning out the light at 3 a.m.

I hope that wasn't too confusing? All that can be added is, first, at least the hotel rooms didn't get trashed; second, it's surprising that England were in a fit state to play any rugby at all, never mind against the All Blacks; and last, before I forget to say, Brown was fined £1,000 for misconduct by the RFU, and Ojo £500.

I'll Give it a Go if You Insist

England v Italy, February 2009

Nick Mallett had a good track record as Springbok coach. A winner of two caps as a player, he oversaw a then-record 17 consecutive Test victories during his time in charge of the national team between 1997 and 2000. A feel for the history of the game does not, however, seem to have been among his attributes, or he might have recalled the fate of South African back row forward Gerrie Sonnekus when he was asked to turn out as scrum-half in the third Test against the 1974 British & Irish Lions (see page 88). If he had, he might have looked for a different solution to the problem facing him as Italy prepared to meet England in the opening game of the 2009 Six Nations.

The problem? All three of Italy's best scrum-halves were injured and only the inexperienced Giulio Toniolatti, with but a single cap to his credit, was available. For whatever reason, Mallett felt unable to risk him at fortress Twickenham. The solution? Go for big-match nous and experience and play Mauro Bergamasco behind the scrum. He was, after all, one of the two or three best Italian players and already a veteran of 69 internationals. How much nous and experience can you reasonably expect? There were one or two minor cracks in this argument. To begin with, a quick, long and accurate pass is appreciated, and an ability to remember that you are playing scrum-half and not open-side flanker is also fairly crucial. Regrettably, both these helpful hints went straight over Mauro's head – as did several of his passes to his fly-half.

Things went wrong from the outset. Within two minutes he was offered an irresistible morsel and dived into the inviting ruck in front of him. The ball went loose, he was not there to take charge of it, England booted it through the gap and into touch ten metres short. Italy overthrew at the lineout and, after a certain amount of faffing about, England recycled the ball and scored the first try.

Oh dear. In case we missed it the first time, Bergamasco gave a repeat performance 15 minutes later. Once again the lure of the ball tempted him into a ruck, leaving Haskell unchallenged in securing it, whipping it out to Ellis and leaving him a clear 20-metre run to the line. Oh dear, oh dear. For his next trick, Mauro tried an overhead pass. It wasn't intended as an overhead pass but it sailed temptingly (for England) over inside centre Garcia's head, for Goode to hack on and Flutey to chase, gather and score. England really were not playing well, seemingly unable to do anything creative on their own account, but were 22–6 up at half-time thanks to Italy's errors. Oh dear, oh dear, oh dear.

At this point, Nick Mallett bowed to the inevitable and hauled poor Mauro off and replaced him with Toniolatti, who showed no inclination to chase the ball into rucks. England staggered unconvincingly to a 36–11 win, though not before the prestige of the Bergamasco family was repaired when brother Mirco on the wing completed a sweeping three-quarter move to score a redemptive try. It was just a shame that Mauro, an outstanding servant of Italian rugby, was subjected to the humiliation of the first half presumably through no choice of his.

'There Is No Glory in Battle Worth the Blood it Costs'

Harlequins v Leinster, Heineken Cup quarter-final, April 2009

It was in the 75th minute that the scandal erupted, with Leinster leading by a single point, 6–5. The scoreline suggests a dour, cautious struggle, but not a bit of it. Rather, as Mick Cleary wrote in the *Telegraph*, 'there was thump and thunder from first to last, toil and shrewdness, and the occasional shimmer...a compelling intensity... all played out before a raucous capacity crowd'. But Quins were a point down with five minutes remaining, a single score needed to capture a semi-final place – just the situation in which Nick Evans, ice-cool master of the dying seconds drop goal or penalty, could be relied on to do the business. The snag was that he'd left the field early in the second half with a poorly knee. How to get him back on?

Coach Dean Richards hatched a cunning plan. A blood injury to one of the Quins' backs would provide the excuse to take one player off and replace him with Evans and, lo and behold, in the aforesaid 75th minute, winger Tom Williams went down with blood issuing from his mouth. Leinster were not best pleased, with Shane Horgan yelling 'it's fake, it's fake', and coach Michael Chelka insisting their doctor be allowed to check for blood, which, according to the rules, was not allowed. Leinster's instincts were right. There was no cut and no blood – just a capsule of not very high quality theatrical blood that had been handed to Williams by physio Steph Brennan during an earlier stoppage. As Williams left the field he was captured on film winking to the bench, and by the time he was back in the dressing room the realisation he might have been rumbled was starting to dawn on him. 'I was quite agitated and nervous,' he later confessed, and sought out team doctor Wendy Chapman to cut his lip in order to produce some real blood. The supreme irony is that, having got Evans onto the field by whatever means, his drop goal attempt from

40 metres with 30 seconds left on the clock failed, so Quins went out of the competition anyway. A small price to pay compared with the furore about to erupt, and continue to rumble throughout the year.

Enquiries soon began. Harlequins initially devised a cover-up plan in which Williams was offered a variety of sweeteners for keeping quiet, including a job when he retired from playing. This resulted in a 12-month playing ban, which, in turn, made Williams seek the advice of the Professional Rugby Players' Association and lawyers were soon involved. He decided that 'I would not allow the club to make me lie again.' Quins Chief Executive Mark Evans and Chairman Charles Jillings outlined the appalling things that could happen to the club and to the individuals involved if the truth came out, including possible relegation from the Premiership, the loss of sponsors and as much as £2 million, quite apart from the severity of individual punishments. But by now it was clear that the truth was emerging, shred by shred, and by the end of August the verdict of a second disciplinary panel had heard enough. Dean Richards, the director of rugby (who had already resigned), was banned for three years, Steph Brennan for two years and the club was fined £260,000. Williams' ban was meanwhile reduced to four months. And all this for a dropped goal attempt that missed.

Invitation to the Ball

Wales v Ireland, Six Nations, March 2011

When their opponents were Irish, Cardiff was in danger of becoming a jinxed venue for Wales. Only once in the previous 28 years had the boys in green lost an international there, and since Wales were on a run of six defeats at the Millennium Stadium the cards looked to be stacked in Ireland's favour once again. As a team they were in for a melodramatic disappointment, and two notable individual achievements, while not passing unnoticed, provided scant consolation. Brian O'Driscoll scored his 24th try to draw level with the championship record, and Ronan O'Gara's conversion and two penalties took him past 1,000 international points and made him only the fifth person to join that elite club.

O'Driscoll's converted try, followed by a couple of O'Gara penalties, looked to have put Ireland on course for the win that kept alive their hopes of a fifth Triple Crown in eight years – though Wales had kept in touch with three penalties of their own. Then, in the 51st minute, came the reverberating clanger. It began uneventfully as Johnny Sexton sliced a clearance kick out of play with his first touch of the ball after coming on as replacement for O'Gara. The pace quickened as a ball boy picked up the nearest ball to hand and gave it to Welsh hooker, Matthew Rees, who took a quick throw-in to Mike Phillips. The scrum-half celebrated his 50th cap by galloping to the line and touching down. The Irish lads were aghast, and with good reason. Rule 19.2(d) states with disarming clarity: 'For a quick throw-in the player must use the ball that went into touch. A quick throw-in is not permitted if another player has touched the ball apart from the player throwing it in and the opponent who carried it into touch. The same team throws into the line-out'. Nice and straightforward with, one would have expected, a clear-cut case of the rule having been broken twice. The ball given to Rees was not the one sliced out by Sexton, and it had been 'contaminated' by the ball boy's touch.

The Irish team 'were in uproar', the *Mail* reported, shouting for the video official to be consulted, and O'Driscoll, as captain, ran to referee Jonathan Kaplan with the same request – a hopeless task, as the rules then in force allowed the TMO to be used only for decisions on the act of scoring. Kaplan pushed O'Driscoll away and asked line judge Peter Allan of Scotland if the correct ball had been used, to which – and he ought to have heard a clanger resonating loud and clear in his head – he replied that it was, and the try was awarded. The Welsh 'try' was converted, and a penalty was awarded later in the game to produce a final result of 13–19 in favour of the home side. As O'Driscoll said after the game: 'We were four points up and in control but Test matches are won and lost on small margins. A moment like that had a huge bearing. They got seven points for it and we lost by six. It's hard to get away from that'. It's not often a bookmaker scrambles onto the moral high ground but Paddy Power did just that, refusing to accept any money for the Welsh win, and returning the £175,000 placed on it.

Up For Grabs

England at the World Cup, September/October 2011

England set out for the 2011 World Cup in New Zealand accompanied by the customary UK press hype that assured us the boys would soon have the trophy back. In the pool stages they ground out uninspiring wins against Georgia and Argentina to clear the way to a quarter-final clash with France, but first a spot of celebration was in order. Right lads, what about a few jars?

Unfortunately they forgot the first rule of the paparazzi and press hounds: get the sensational headline and worry about the facts later – if at all. First, there was the provocative circumstance that England skipper Mike Tindall was newly engaged to Zara Phillips, daughter of Princess Anne, so if only they could catch him, in particular, up to no good Christmas would have come early. World Cup and royal family scandal all in one – joy and bliss. Mike Tindall duly obliged. Through a glass porthole in the door of the Altitude Bar pictures were taken of some of the players 'in extremely relaxed mood'. At this point, according to that reliable source, the *Sun*, 'scores of women made a beeline for the lads'. So what's unusual and where does Mike Tindall figure in the scene? We're getting to that.

'One particularly beautiful blonde went straight for Mike. But rather than reject her advances, unfortunately' (said the *Sun*, hinting at the moral high ground) 'he was extremely responsive... she pulled his head towards her breasts and she rubbed the back of his head as she did so.' The woman in question was later identified as his ex-girlfriend Jessica Parker, which, while it made a difference, it was only by a degree or two given that he had just become engaged to somebody else. But while it gave the media a gift-wrapped story there was more to come.

Not only was Mike flirting with a blonde (who was, naturally, not only blonde but 'gorgeous') but he was doing so, it seemed, while engaged in 'a dwarf-throwing contest'. This must have been true because even the *Daily Mail* agreed that it was so, although Rich Deane, manager of the Altitude Bar where the vertically-challenged persons were allegedly being tossed about, seemed less certain. 'There was no dwarf-throwing. That's just not cool!' he said. 'There was no scandal by any of the English rugby players that we saw. They were great lads, not throwing the midgets, it was all light-hearted, good humoured fun!' Ah-ha! So *somebody* was tossing midgets about, then, but not the English lads? It's all rather confusing, especially as none of the paparazzi seem to have managed any photos of under-sized people in mid-air. But one fact was incontestable. Once the World Cup was over, Tindall was fined £25,000 and thrown out of the England elite player squad, never to regain his place. *The Times* surmised that this unprecedented punishment may have been because Tindall refused to admit any guilt, thereby forcing manager Martin Johnson to defend him.

If, by now, Johnson was starting to wonder why he had accepted the manager's job in the first place, worse was to come barely a fortnight later. 'Hotel-room scandal rocks World Cup bid,' shrieked the *Mail*, as James Haskell, Chris Ashton and Dylan Hartley were alleged to have 'inappropriately' harassed a female hotel employee down in Dunedin. Poor old Martin J barely knew what to say as this second storm broke. 'It's not great (for England's image), that is why I'm angry with the players – those three,' and he went on to repeat that, however angry he was, he had to trust them. Two of the three, Haskell and Ashton, were subsequently each fined £5,000.

If Johnno anticipated redemption on the pitch his hopes were quickly dashed. England had promised to 'blitz' the French in the first 20 minutes of their quarter-final, but it was France who launched the blitzkrieg. England made one error after another, surrendering both penalties and tries to be 16–0 down at the break. They were in disarray, and only Yachvili's wayward kicking prevented a worse deficit. England had never before clawed back a 12-point deficit, let alone 16; and although a quick tap and go from Ben Youngs as the final quarter loomed opened the way for Foden to touch down and Wilkinson to convert, continued errors and wasted possession underlined their hopeless position. A dropped goal from Yachvili widened the gap again, and Mark Cueto's try in the closing moments did no more than disguise the magnitude of the beating in the final 19–12 scoreline. Johnson's contract was due to expire a few weeks after the World Cup exit, but, following a month of scandals mixed with disappointment on the pitch, he had had enough, and stepped down.

'We Didn't Turn Up'

Wales v England, March 2013

As embarrassments go, this was on a seismic scale for England. They arrived in Cardiff primed for the Grand Slam with their own media hyping their chances in customary fashion. Wales, meantime, having endured eight straight losses in a miserable summer and autumn of 2012, had rediscovered their inspiration and, if they could win by eight points, would be champions. The teams came out to a wall of sound that scarcely abated throughout the match. When the anthems were sung before kickoff the crowd of 74,104 won the contest approximately 74,000 to 104, and the rugby followed much the same pattern. 'We didn't turn up,' said England manager Stuart Lancaster after the game. Had it been literally true it would have been a pity because, no matter the result, they would have missed a crackerjack of a game.

As the Sky commentator said, the 'bone-crunching first half was played at 100 miles per hour for 40 minutes,' no quarter being asked or given. No tries were scored, but quite a few penalties were given as it rapidly became apparent that the Welsh pack was dominating the scrums and the rucks. Steve Walsh is a referee whose whims at the set piece are frequently mystifying, but on this occasion there could be no querying a penalty count that was firmly in Wales's favour. 9–3 to the home side at half-time, and the noise level unabated as the crowd began to anticipate a Welsh victory.

The anticipation was fully justified. Whatever may have been said in the England dressing room at half-time, it didn't work. On 50 minutes Leigh Halfpenny slotted a fourth penalty and then, six minutes later, the crowd got what it had wanted from the outset. Whatever their other failings, the English defence of its line had been impregnable until Alex Cuthbert got the ball in enough space to give him a glimpse of the corner. He pinned his ears back and went for it, comfortably evading Mike Brown's attempt at a tap-tackle. Just to make sure the margin would comfortably exceed the eight points required, Dan Biggar dropped a goal eight minutes later, and only 60 seconds after that the icing was firmly laid on the cake. Sam Warburton broke from a scrum, drew two defenders and beat them both before feeding the ball down the line where Justin Tipuric carried it on, drawing the defenders on to him before slipping the most skilful of passes to Cuthbert for his second try.

The final score was a more than emphatic 30–3, and the Championship was in Welsh hands. 'Wales thoroughly deserved the win,' said Stuart Lancaster. There was not much else he could say in the face of what amounted to humiliation for a side aspiring to the Grand Slam, and to his credit he made no attempt to find excuses. Wales were understandably jubilant. 'This is better than the Grand Slam last year,' said interim coach Rob Howley, with every justification, since Wales had secured back-to-back championships for the first time since the glory days of 1979. Another quite remarkable statistic: the old rivalry of England v Wales had at this point been ignited 124 times. Twelve of those games had been drawn, and of the remainder each side had won 56. There is no other contest in rugby that can boast such equality. Long may it continue.

'Not in the Wildest Dreams...'

Saracens v Clermont, April 2014

Clermont Auvergne were widely touted as the best club side in Europe as they prepared for their Heineken Cup semi-final against Saracens at Twickenham. There was good reason for the accolade. Throughout the earlier stages of the competition they had been devastating in disposing of the opposition, with as much ease away from home as in their own fortress stadium – and they rode high in the Top 14 to boot. Mind you, it never crossed the Saracens' mind-set that they were the underdogs. After all, they were top of the Premiership and had visibly improved in the 12 months since their defeat by Toulon in the 2013 Heineken semis. Expecting a huge crowd for this titanic clash the game was scheduled for Twickenham, so it was disappointing that fewer than 26,000 turned up but – as Eddie Butler noted in *The Observer* – at least it meant the sound of the Vunipolas, Mako and Billy, making contact carried to all seats.

The match certainly was a titanic clash, but not in the sense of a tense, even struggle with the result in doubt to the last minute of injury time. In the event Sarries tore into Clermont with the ferocity of a tornado. 'Never have the Michelin men from the Auvergne... been bullied into utter submission as they were here' reported *The Guardian*. The Saracens forwards like to call themselves the Wolf Pack and there was certainly a call of the wild about the way they enforced a formidable defence of the ball, led by the southern Africans at the heart of the pack – Schalk Brits, Mouritz Botha and, in particular, Jacques Burger. The 'widow-maker' (to give him one of his dressing-room nicknames) actually touched the ball just twice in the 70 minutes he was on the pitch, but in that time he delivered 28 frenzied tackles to secure possession for his own side, and very good use they made of it.

Chris Ashton, having one of his sharpest games in many months, started the rout with the first of his two tries, and in such serious mood was he that he forsook his customary swallow-dive to touch down and made do with what was described as 'a demi-swallow.' Clermont pulled back a penalty to make it 7–3, which was as close as they were to get to a victory. With a quarter of an hour gone, Mako Vunipola charged down Lee Byrne's attempted clearance, the ball bounced into Clermont's in-goal area and as Sarrie centre Marcelo Bosch challenged Brock James for the touch down, James palmed the ball over the dead-ball line, whereupon referee Nigel Owens awarded a penalty try and flourished a yellow card to rub in the general sinfulness of the deed.

This was on the harsh side, but was it a clanger? There was much Gallic muttering and shaking of heads at the injustice of it all, convinced as they were that James had really only meant to push the ball out of Bosch's reach. Maybe or maybe not, but the French have long suspected British referees of an incurable bias against them, and ten minutes later that conviction probably felt confirmed when a Clermont try was disallowed for obstruction on Owen Farrell by flanker Damien Chouly. If there was such a thing in this game as a turning point this was probably it. By half-time the score stood at 24–6 with Saracens already three tries to the good, and by the time Clermont staggered off the field at the final whistle it was 46–6. Had the real clanger been dropped by Clermont in underestimating the ability of their own hardened pack to withstand the ferocity of their opponents and prepare accordingly? Whether or not it was the case, the winning margin of 40 points, and the try tally of six to nothing, were the largest in Heineken semi-finals' history. As Eddie Butler wrote: 'Not in the dreams of the most ardent fez-wearing fan could this have been seen coming.'

True, but nor could Saracens' defeat a week or two later to Toulon in the final, and to Northampton Saints in the Premiership playoff. Their performance against Clermont had been magnificent but, in the end, they were unable to summon up a repeat.

'Epic Showpiece'
Decided by a Howler

Crusaders v Waratahs, Super Rugby Final, August 2014

These days there's the suspicion of a developing trend in rugby towards one of soccer's least appealing aspects – that of the coach or manager blaming the referee for everything that went against his (losing) team. Rugby is a fast game with a complex set of rules and regulations. By and large professional referees do a good job and players generally accept their decisions without question, even when they may think a bloomer's been made or a clanger dropped. Mind you, the potential for being penalised and shunted back ten metres for arguing or questioning the ref's vision is a good incentive for maintaining law and order. That said, referees do make occasional mistakes, and this book has gleefully chronicled a number of them, so it is refreshing when authority dons the mantle of Gwyn Nicholls in 1909 (see page 92) and owns up and apologises, albeit too late to repair the damage inflicted.

The poor referee whose name in Christchurch, New Zealand, is currently muddier than the muddiest third fifteen pitch is Craig Joubert, who may think himself lucky that he comes from South Africa and therefore resides a very long way from the scene of his blooper. The context of the 'epic showpiece' of which he was in charge was the Allianz Stadium in Sydney, which hosted the Super Final of the southern hemisphere season between the Waratahs and the Crusaders. The latter were rather good at this event, having won it on seven occasions, whereas the Waratahs were virgins, despite two previous Final appearances in 2005 and 2008, their nemesis on both occasions being – yes, you've guessed it – the Crusaders.

Throughout the season the Waratahs' trade mark had been all-out attack from the first whistle, while the Crusaders had been slow burners, seemingly having to shake themselves into top gear, and the opening salvoes of the Final followed this pattern. Within three minutes indiscipline gave the Waratahs a penalty, followed almost at once by a sweeping back line move finished by Adam Ashley-Cooper as he broke through three tackles for an unconverted try. 8–0 inside five minutes, and 14–0 soon after, which, at last, provoked the Crusaders into upping their discipline and their intensity. Kieran Read engineered their opening try, Carter converted, and the two sides traded penalties to make the half-time score 20–13 to the Waratahs.

If the Crusaders had started the match slowly, it was not a mistake they repeated after the restart as they levelled the scores with a brilliant winger's try from Nadolo and a fine touchline conversion by Slade, who had taken over the kicking duties when Dan Carter was injured in his first match back from a seven month lay-off. More penalties kept the scoreboard in business and with 25 minutes remaining the Crusaders led narrowly, 26–23. The tension and determination were visibly ratcheting up, and when Ashley-Cooper snaffled a Kurtley Beale offload to burst through for his second try, this time converted, the Waratahs were ahead 30–26. Provided they kept their line intact they were, surely, just about home and dry? No way. Four minutes later another penalty made it 30–29, and with just three minutes left the Crusaders won a further penalty to lead 30–32 with the game all but done.

Cue Craig Joubert's big moment. From the restart a ruck developed between halfway and the Crusader's 22-metre line, with 110 seconds remaining. Mr Joubert stood over it watchfully as the ball began to come back on the Waratahs' side. One of their forwards seized it and broke around the ruck to be tackled by Richie McCaw who'd been hovering behind the ruck anticipating just such a move. Plainly nothing illegal had taken place, but suddenly the referee's arm was up and McCaw was pinged for 'entering the ruck illegally'. The penalty was 35 metres out, fairly straight and, almost inevitably, it sailed over to give the Waratahs their first title, 33–32. To his eternal credit McCaw didn't succumb to hysteria or question the injustice of it all, just turned with the slightest shake of the head and walked back to the goal line to await the coup de grace. It was an almost inexplicable decision. Top sportsmen sometimes talk of brains being scrambled by the non-stop concentration demanded of a fast, tight contest, to the point where you can fail to grasp things that would earlier be second nature. That something similar happened to Craig Joubert seems the only explanation for what happened.

He knew it was a howler. Next morning he phoned Todd Blackadder, the Crusaders' coach and, in McCaw's words, 'put his hand up' admitting he'd made a wrong call that probably cost his team their eighth crown. That took courage.

'I Was a Bit Puzzled and Bemused'

Sydney Stars v North Harbour Rays, Australian National Championship, October 2014

'A bit puzzled and bemused' is something of an understatement, and photos of the incident confirm that such a look transfused the handsome features of Rays' forward Mitch Lewis as he discovered he'd been credited with rugby's first-ever recorded case of an own try. In soccer, own goals occur with splendid regularity and can even include elegant strikes from way out, but an own try? Sad to say, the one in question was not a dashing, dummy-selling, side-stepping sprint for the wrong line. Such panache might at least have brought cheers of admiration, if only from the other side. But no, this was a blunder of the shove and grunt variety – and in truth it didn't really happen, except for the unarguable fact that the try in question remains in the official scorebook.

It all happened in the 21st minute of the game, with the Stars rucking furiously on the Rays' line. Lewis was battling away in there as a good forward should, and managed to rip the ball out of the opposing hooker's hands. As he explained later 'I had possession and went to place it, and as I was placing it back I wasn't sure if I should put it over the line. I thought it would be a five-metre scrum and I thought that would be the safest option.' Video footage shows him doing just that – he is over the ball, left arm reaching under him and between his legs, hand – and only his hand – planted firmly on the ball. Cue the referee, and I'm afraid it's the official who's going to cop it yet again. There really is too much of this going on, but when another clanger is there in front of us we just have to grin and bear it.

The referee called in the TMO, and after brief deliberation back came the verdict: try, scored by James Willan, the hooker from whose grasp Lewis had wrested the ball.

What had happened? The confusion seems to have arisen because of the colour yellow. The Stars play in yellow shirts with yellow quarter-length sleeves, whereas the Rays are colourfully kitted out in green, blue, red and white but – crucially – with yellow quarter-length sleeves, and yes, you've guessed it. The TMO saw a flash of yellow and assumed it was on Willan's arm rather than that of its rightful owner, poor old Mitch Lewis. So try, or rather own try, given. Good news? Stars missed the conversion. Bad news? Rays lost the game 49–40. Still, Lewis will be bought a lot of the amber nectar (poor soul) in future in return for telling the story of the first 'own try'.

Not So Easy, Pisi

Racing Metro v Northampton Saints, European Champions Cup, October 2014

Just how red-faced can a man get? Soccer fans are well used to the sight of a striker fluffing a gift and collapsing to the ground clutching a knee or some other part of the anatomy to excuse his errant ways. It can happen in rugby, too – just ask Fiji's Severo Koroduadua (see page 106). But first let's put this particular costly embarrassment into proper context. It was the opening day of the 2014/15 European Champions Cup, and by common consent away teams, if they couldn't force a win, must at least come away with a losing bonus point in a competition that had nudged a further rung up the ladder of toughness with the demise of its predecessor, the Heineken Cup.

For most of the game Saints, the reigning English champions, had been below their best, outscrummaged by Racing in the set pieces, finding lineout ball difficult to secure, getting slow ball from the rucks, and therefore being unable to create space for their lively backs to break down the opposing defence. After Racing's early converted try it became a continuous slog to hold their own line and keep themselves in contention in the hope of opportunities as the fourth quarter came in sight. In this at least they were succeeding. Down 10–3 at the break, an early second half penalty brought them to within four points, and Racing's loss of prop Brugnaut to the sin bin (questionably, it has to be said, but can you ever understand what goes on in the depths of the scrum?) promised an opportunity for Northampton to open gaps. And this is exactly what they achieved as their usually lethal outside centre George Pisi intercepted a pass on the 22 and sped in under the posts – or rather *almost* under the posts. With five paces to go, and the opposition nowhere, the ball suddenly squirted from under his right arm and dropped to the turf a split second before he joined it, clutching his thigh. Seven points gone in spectacular fashion – hilarious for the Racing fans, head in hands time for those of the Saints. A torn hamstring was the speculation as he was helped from the field, but whatever the cause a potential lead of 13–10 remained obstinately 10–6 against the visitors, and shortly became 13–6 as Racing landed another penalty.

Nil desperandum. Northampton kept on trying and, helped by a second yellow card, this time against Ben Amus in the back row, Phil Dowson finally forced his way over in the corner in the 75th minute. 13–11 and the hitherto impeccable Stephen Myler to convert. Two points for the draw beckoned bewitchingly and, with a few minutes still left, who knows, maybe a penalty or drop goal for victory? But Myler missed, and by some distance. Oh well, guys, we'll just have to settle for the losing bonus point. It could be worse. But it could. From the restart Racing did the obvious and made sure the remaining play took place in Northampton's third of the pitch, mauling and driving relentlessly until, as the clock went red, Saints dropped the second clanger. They turned the ball over, but instead of taking it back into contact to win possession and give their kicker more time to boot it out, Myler flung it to Ben Foden, whose hurried kick was charged down and over the try line for Andreu to fall on it. 18–11, and Goosen's touchline conversion was as divinely perfect as Myler's had been wickedly wayward only a few moments earlier. 20–11 to Racing, so Northampton, who at different points in the game might have secured 4, 2 or 1 point(s) came away with nowt. In the aftermath the Saints' dressing room language must have been ungodly.

Is This a Ball I See Before Me?
Come, Let me Clutch Thee!

England v New Zealand, November 2014

Stuart Lancaster probably had sharp words for Mike Brown after the game, but if Mike had been Macbeth they would have been as nothing to the earful Lady Macbeth would have conjured up for him.

We were spared the usual patriotic media breast-thumping during the week before kickoff. After all, England had been decisively beaten on the June tour to the land of the long white cloud, so the English mood was more an air of cautious optimism with breath tightly held. Was this to be the 'new' England, demonstrating its readiness for World Cup glory eleven months down the road? For ten spectacular minutes it looked as if the answer might be yes; for the next thirty...... well, possibly; and for the whole of the second half, emphatically no chance. The final All Black victory 21–24 flattered England well beyond their deserving.

Yet those first ten minutes were both exhilarating and frustrating. With the game only three minutes old, Jonny May scored as spectacular a try as Twickenham has seen in a decade. England won quick ball from a ruck 10 metres inside the All Black half, and it went swiftly from Danny Care to Owen Farrell to Brad Barritt, who timed his pass beautifully to May as he hit the line at speed. And what speed! On a slightly angled run, he took Conrad Smith on the outside, swerved inside Ben Smith and, as Israel Dagg swept across, confident of intercepting him, rounded him on the outside as well to touch down. The Blacks are not used to having their cover shredded like this, and were as shocked as Twickenham was ecstatic.

England continued to attack, recycling at pace and maintaining the pressure. Four minutes later May was in the thick of it again, following up and gathering a kick into the 22 with Farrell unmarked inside him and the line beckoning. A quick release would have seen a second try, but May delayed a split second too long and this time Dagg nailed him, so a chance that should have been taken was wasted. Three minutes later and it looked for all the world as if everything would be forgiven. England were once again attacking inside the New Zealand 22 and Kyle Eastmond, spotting the yawning gap on the right wing, sent a perfect long pass for Mike Brown to run onto and score with the undefended line at his mercy. The crowd was already up on its feet in celebration of a copper-bottomed try, but... but he dropped it. Why? Eye off the ball? Looking for non-existent All Black defenders? Thinking of which victory dive to use? Who can say why, but, lacking Macbeth's killer instinct, he failed to clutch it.

Instead of being at least 15, if not 19, points to the good, England were squandering chances in a way international sides aspiring to be top class cannot afford. Instead of being rattled and on the back foot, the Blacks scored their first try only three minutes later. Had it not been for their woeful goal kicking, which saw 12 points squandered with kicks that verged on the embarrassing, New Zealand would have been comfortably ahead at half-time. As it was, Farrell's three penalties meant England took a slender lead of 14–11 back to the dressing room.

Could England, in the second half, recreate the forward momentum, rapid possession and quick handling of the first ten minutes? They could not. As Kieran Read said afterwards: 'They started really well, then maybe went away from their strength. They scored a great try by passing the ball but later on they closed up a bit.' This was a tactful understatement. England barely got out of their own half in the last 40 minutes, conceding two tries in the process. It wasn't that they went away from their forward strength, which was impressive throughout, but that they then reverted to a poorly executed kicking game, repeatedly surrendering possession instead of finding space. Apart from killing their own momentum it enabled Charlie Faumuina to score the Blacks' third, brilliant try after 22 phases of possession. That the England pack forced New Zealand to concede a penalty try in the closing seconds merely hinted at undeserved respectability, and we were left to wonder what might have been if those first ten minutes had yielded the three tries of which only one was scored.

It's That ******* Goalpost Again!

Wales v England, Six Nations, February 2015

England have taken a bit of a panning in the last few sections of this book, so for their supporters it's a relief to be able to celebrate good news, especially after a decidedly shaky opening ten minutes. Before we even get to that, a packed stadium, not to mention myriad TV-watchers, had to endure a pre-match build-up that verged on the infantile, the lowlight being a DJ called Spoony. *The Guardian* was far from alone in its scorn: 'must rank among the worst, most superfluous bookings in sporting history,' was its tart comment. When will those responsible for these shenanigans get it into their heads that big rugby matches create a fantastic atmosphere all of their own? They don't need, and indeed suffer from, this artificial hype.

Luckily a terrific game of rugby soon blew away the after-effects, and Welsh supporters enjoyed an almost perfect start. In the seventh minute, Taulupe Faletau broke from the back of a scrum that England were shoving backwards at speed and beat James Haskell, whose feeble attempt at a choke tackle allowed him to put Rhys Webb in for a try. England's front five were unlikely to have seen the funny side. With Halfpenny converting, and adding a penalty three minutes later, England were already 10–0 to the bad, and their fans were beginning to have nightmares about a repetition of the 2013 game (see page 176). But in the 14th minute, a clever little grubber kick from Mike Brown into Anthony Watson's path saw the winger race in for a try, giving notice that the fight back had begun. By the 40th minute, penalties had seen the score increase to 13–8 in Wales's favour and then, with the clock in the red zone, Dan Biggar dropped a beauty of a goal from deep to make it 16–8 at half-time. As it transpired those were the last points the Welsh would register.

It would be wrong to suggest that England were transformed in the second half, but the intensity with which the momentum of attack was maintained gave them, step by step, domination of the proceedings. They were on the front foot almost from the start of the half, spurred on by a magical try from Jonathan Joseph in the 44th minute. From around the 22 he broke away from Biggar's tackle and pirouetted through two would-be blockers to spin back towards the posts and touch down. 16–8 had become 16–15, and thanks to resolute Welsh defence so it remained for the next quarter-hour until Haskell endured the second of the moments he would rather erase from an otherwise fine performance.

With an uncanny replication of Hal Sever's notorious encounter 77 years earlier (see page 56) he broke for the line at full speed, aiming to touch down beneath the crossbar, only to encounter an all-too-solid goalpost instead. Baldly stated, it sounds funny, but whereas Sever did not have the benefit of television to provide endless replays, we are able to reconstruct Haskell's problem as often as we wish. Just as Sever knew perfectly well where both post and try line were but was forced onto the post by defenders fore and aft, so Haskell was taken simultaneously by Faletau from behind and Alex Cuthbert head on and spun round onto the post. One might argue that even so he should have had the wit to sidestep the post and force his way over and down, but this is an armchair argument. In any case the referee was playing advantage, so the penalty was there for the taking. It was, and England led for the first time.

In the 74th minute, Dave Attwood went over for a third try, but was disallowed for obstruction three phases earlier, and so it was left to George Ford to stroke over a further penalty to put the issue beyond doubt. An outstanding match – tense, skilful and full of passion from both sides. Even the goalpost was tempted to jump up and cheer.

About the Author

David Mortimer is a lifelong rugby and cricket enthusiast who, despite years of sweaty endeavour, never became good enough to perform before more than about twenty-five people (dogs included). The many clangers he perpetrated therefore never received the wider recognition he felt they deserved. To compensate he continues to follow both sports avidly, dispensing lungfuls of helpful advice from touchline or sofa – but with great fellow-feeling for the careless or unintended moment that provokes derision or disbelief.